THE ARCHANGEL APOTHECARY:

INCENSE, OILS, HERBS, POTIONS, & PRAYERS FOR EVERYDAY LIFE

BY Dar Payment

2017

DAP Publications

Lake Elsinore, California 92532-2523 U.S.A

THE ARCHANGEL APOTHECARY; Incense, Oils, Herbs, Potions & Prayers for Everyday Life

ISBN-13: 978-1974432974
ISBN-10: 1974432971

Dedication

To my team of Angels . . . I love you so much!

To my beloved groom Michael. Thank you for your support, encouragement, and boundless love. I am the luckiest woman in the world!

And last, but not least, to my sister Maya. Thank you for just being you.

Table of Contents

Introduction

For thousands of years our ancestors have used the healing magic of herbs in ointments, elixirs, potions, sachets, and incense.

Throughout the centuries, herbal recipes for health and wholeness were passed down from healer to healer; many which were kept secret and recorded in the journals of the "wise ones", who were the men, women, priests, priestess, and shamans, all of whom were skilled in the art of herbal healing and herbal lore.

This is also true with certain traditions of herbal folk lore, and folk magic; such as that of hoodoo, vodoun, and other spiritual earth traditions who harnessed the healing and transformative power of herbs, elixirs, and oils.

Today in the modern 21st-century the veil of secrecy no longer exists. And for many, the use of herbs and essential oils offers and effective, and holistic approach to physical health, and emotional wellness.

The recipes shared in this book have their roots from both traditional herbal medicine and herbal folk lore, as well as from that of certain folk magic traditions.

As a New Thought minister, Angel Intuitive with over 30+ years of professional experience, and as a lay herbalist and aromatherapy practitioner; I stand by the recipes and prayers shared in this book. They have been used with great success by my personal clients, and they will work for you as well.

Please note that this book is not about worshiping Angels, but it is about discovering how work with the Archangels by learning how to harness their unique energy attributes to create health, wealth, and wholeness in all areas of your life.

It is also important to note that no one spiritual tradition owns the angelic realm. Angels are a very present help for everyone everywhere.

A wise man once said, "The best way to truly become intimate with herbs and their "magic" is to work with them."

This means to experiment with them and to let them show you their effectiveness.

 Despite the criticism from those who practice a more traditional approach to Western medicine, herbal healing has been proven to be effective. This is because herbal healing is natural in that it's only tools are those given to you by nature; as a precious gift from Universal Love.

I believe that all paths lead to God. And whether you choose to address the Higher Spiritual Power as the Holy Spirit, Divine Source, or Universal Oneness, or by any other name, what is important to remember is that God and the Angels love you and want you to live a healthy, whole, and complete life full of every good thing. This is your right as a divine child of the Universe.

Blessings, Love, and Light,

Dar Payment

Warning and Disclaimer

The author of this book is not a medical doctor. Information shared in this book is for educational purposes only and is not intended to diagnose, treat, cure, or prevent any disease, and has not been evaluated by the FDA.

Also, the information provided in this book is not intended to be a substitute for medical treatment. If you're under the care of a physician or taking prescription medications, please always check with your physician before using essential oils and herbs in any form. It is our intention that your experience with the recipes shared in this book is safe and enjoyable.

Take special care in researching your own needs and the needs of your family when considering the various uses of essential oils and herbs. Special precautions should be taken for those pregnant and nursing, as well as for children. If you are pregnant or nursing do not use the recipes suggested in this book without consulting a qualified physician.

Trust your intuition, do you research, and never use any essential oils or herbs in a way which makes you feel uncomfortable.

On Herbal Lore, & Folk Magic

This is not a book on "magic" and I do not consider these recipes to be "magic". I believe that you and I create our own magic in life through our positive thoughts and intentions. I will share more about this in an upcoming section of this chapter.

The physical sciences teach us that everything is made of energy. And what I find interesting to note is that plants and herbs have been found to have their own unique energy vibrations that can be seen and measured through scientific mediums such as Kirlian Photography, and Electrophysiology, as well as through more holistic methods such as muscle testing.

The energy signatures of plants and herbs can be amplified when mixed together, as well as through imbuing the ingredients with your own bioenergetic energy, known in the East as chi, as well as through focused prayer.

The archangels also have their own unique energy vibration. When you imbue these energy vibrations with a specific intention, and through prayer, the result is like a mega power magnet. Your wants, needs, and desires, can and most often do manifest into your life quickly and easily.

Candles, incense, and oils which are in harmony with your intended goal, also add a quasi-ritual component to your energy workings. Not only does the use of these ingredients contribute their own energies to your intentions, but they also help you create a slight hypnotic trance by shifting your brain wave patterns to what is called the alpha state.

When you are in the alpha state you are very susceptible to suggestion. The media moguls know this and spend hundreds of thousands of dollars each year researching how to quickly influence what you and I buy.

When performing a specific rite or ritual the alpha brain wave state is quite advantageous as it causes your intentions to bypass your conscious sensor; carrying your emotionally charged desires directly into your subconscious mind. Your subconscious mind is also known as the genie of your mind. Its mantra is 'your wish is my command'; and it always acts upon your highly charged thoughts, beliefs, and desires, whether they are positive or negative.

Now a quick word about rituals. A ritual is simply a set routine or method for carrying out a specific task. Fundamentalist religions perform rituals all the time. For the purpose of this book a 'ritual' or rite simply means the suggested ways to use your personal bioenergetic energy along with the energy of the archangels, and your desired intention, combined with one of the specific recipes of need shared with you throughout the pages of this book.

In my opinion, a ritual, or rite, is simply what I call, active prayer. Everything performed in your rituals will be unique to you and your desire or need. There is no set way to do things, so make your rites, rituals, or active prayers, simple and fun.

This book is a compendium of herbal processes and recipes. Though these mixtures contain certain energies in and of themselves, they are far more effective when used in conjunction with the suggested simple ritual methods outlined in this book.

A Little More on Magic

In the past magic was considered to be a process of combining the power of natural energies together in order to achieve a desired result or goal.

Throughout the ages, human beings have experienced the invisible forces around them; such as electricity, the effects of magnetism, gravity, as well as the energy from their own bioenergetic system.

Ancient astronomers and astrologers also discovered and documented the energetic effects of other planets on the earth, as well as those effects on the human body. A great example of this is the effect the full moon has on the female biological systems, as well as that of the general populace.

My father was fond of reading the Sunday paper. And as a child, I remember at least one time each month hearing my dad call out to my mother, "Must be a full moon coming Jody. All the crazies are out!"

Without a scientific understanding of universal law and the physical sciences, our ancient ancestors coined the term "magic" to describe these unknown forces. Today, we understand the magic our ancestors often spoke of, to be natural effects that can be explained through the physical sciences such as those in the disciplines of quantum physics, brain sciences, and universal law.

Universal law, more particularly the Law of Attraction, teaches us that thoughts are things. Continuous emotionally charged thoughts have a magnetic pull and can and will create results based upon your projected thoughts whether positive or negative.

Quantum physics teaches that everything is energy, and has its own unique energy vibration or signature. When combining the energy signatures with those of the archangels, herbs, plants, etc. you are able to raise and amplify their energy vibrations when you merge them with your specific intention; and then activating that with emotionally charged thoughts, words, or prayers.
In my mind, that is truly magical!

Your Karmic Responsibility

When creating and using the recipes shared in this book it is your karmic responsibility to always do so from a place of integrity and love.

Never use any of these recipes to try to force or bend another to your will. This is especially true with the recipes that are intended to make you more magnetic in love and relationships.

Working with the archangels is an outflow of the highest form of Love. Love can never go against Love. If your intentions are to control or manipulate someone else you're actually working against love and the Angels cannot and will not support you.

The basic rule of thumb is to always ensure that your intention is for the highest benefit of all concerned.

The Power of Intention

Your intention is your particular need or goal. Love. Money. Health. Protection. These are all a set goal or intention.

Your goal or intention is what sets the Law of Attraction in motion. Clarity is key when activating the Law of Attraction, and your specific goal or intention is the ignition. Without these two ingredients, the Law of Attraction cannot be consciously activated in your behalf.

Directing Your Personal Energy

Directing your personal energy means two things. First, it means owning your personal power which is the energy you use to create your direct experience. Your personal power is your ability to choose how you wish to think, believe, and feel in any given situation.

Second, directing your personal energy means harnessing your own innate life force. This life force is a natural extension of your bioenergetic body.

In Oriental medicine traditions, this energy is called chi. Acupuncturists, Taoist Masters, and martial artists have long understood the value and power of chi. There are many documented studies of amazing and mind-boggling feats by those skilled in moving and directing their chi.

Those practiced in the energy healing arts such as Reiki, Healing Touch, the Universal Healing Art of Jing-Qi-Shen, etc., all understand how to draw upon and send this energy during their healing sessions.

You will learn how to direct your own personal energy in the next chapter of this book. Learning how to do so is an important and valuable skill. Because when you learn to combine your personal energy with the herbs and plants corresponding to the recipes in this book, you will be able to supercharge your overall results. The higher your vibrational resonance is, the quicker you will magnetize your results.

Creating a Sacred Working Space

To create and work with these recipes you will need to create sacred space. Many people call their sacred working space their altar. It does not matter what you choose to call it. What does matter is that this place is an area where will you be undisturbed.

Your sacred working space can be anywhere - your kitchen table, bathroom counter, coffee table, etc. It can be indoors, or outdoors.

The most important thing to remember when selecting your sacred space is that focused prayer requires your full attention, so make sure you perform all of your workings in an area will you will not be disturbed by people or pets for an hour or so.

Your sacred space can be as simple or as ornate as you'd like it to be. If you want to dress it up with a cloth covering, gemstones and crystals, flowers, candles, or incense, feel free to do so it's entirely up to you.

I prefer my sacred working space to be simple. As a matter of fact, my sacred working space is often the kitchen table. I purchased an inexpensive bamboo placemat and a 12 x 12 ceramic tile from the hardware store. I find this to be a perfect, and resilient working area, and when using the ceramic tile, I never have to worry about my herbs, oils, or candle wax ruining anything.

Basic Tools and Supplies

Along with a sacred working space, you will also need to have the following basic supplies. Most of these can be found around the house, purchased online, or purchased at your local Walmart, or Target stores.

- A ceramic pan for simmering potpourri and tea
- A small and medium ceramic or glass bowl for mixing
- A set of measuring spoons
- A one or two cup glass measuring cup
- A set of dry measuring cups
- An incense censer for burning incense
- An essential oil diffuser
- Eye droppers for measuring oils
- Self-igniting charcoal blocks for burning loose incense

- Small bags or pouches for herbal sachets
- Candles and holders (my preference is to use novena jar candles or tea lights)
- Various sizes of glass jars to store your mixtures
- Small glass spritzer bottles
- Disposable paper towels to help clean up accidental spills

The Basic Ritual

So how do you put together a basic ritual with the archangel's help? To be honest there is no set way to use the recipes outlined in this book. The basic ritual shared with you in the following paragraphs is a general guideline, one that not only I follow, but also my clients. Why? Because it provides results!

Also remember not to get too hung up on the word ritual. Once again, for the purposes of this book, a ritual is simply a moving or active prayer.

Note: you don't need to perform the outlined ritual. If you just want to make a particular recipe go for it! As I said previously, there are no set rules when it comes to using the recipes outlined in this book.

1. Set your intention. What is the goal or result you wish to bring into your life experience? Love? Healing? Money? A new home? A new job? Be very clear about what it is that you want. Remember your intention is always the springboard for the Law of Attraction.

2. Choose a recipe that lines up with your goal. For example, let's say your intention is to find another job. You would search the recipes in this book for those that are designed for that particular purpose. For this example, we will choose the Archangel Chamuel Job Finder Charm. Please note that you may also choose to use two or three recipes the correspond with your goal simultaneously.

3. Gather the necessary supplies and required ingredients. Having everything ready to go and at hand helps you to avoid distraction, allowing you to focus on the task at hand instead of stopping periodically to find a measuring cup, tea ball, spoon, etc.

4. Choose a prayer that corresponds with the Archangel responsible for that goal. For our example, we see that the Archangel that matches our goal is Archangel Chamuel; commonly known as the "Finder" Archangel. Turn to the section in this book on prayers, and select the prayer that best resonates with you and also with that of your goal. Once again, there are no set rules here. If you choose to use your own prayer feel free to do so.

5. Set up your sacred space. Light a candle, burn some incense, play some soft meditative music in the background, or do whatever you feel would blend the angel's subtle energy vibrations with your ritual.

6. Bring all the ingredients together. Follow the recipe and measure and combine the ingredients as instructed. Stay present while you do this. Don't allow your mind to wander off. This would be a good time for you to feel the great feelings of what it would be like if you have already achieved your desired goal. See and visualize your results as if you have already achieved them. This is a powerful way to activate the Law of Attraction.

7. Bless the finished recipe with love and light, and then repeat the corresponding prayer to God and the Archangel. Blessing the finished recipe is also called charging it. I will share with you how to do that in the next chapter. Charging the finished recipe is a very important step in this process as infuses and lifts up the energy signature of the ingredients you used with that of your personal energy vibration, as well as with that of your intention. After you have blessed your recipe and offered your prayer of desire or need you are ready to use your recipe.

8. Wash, rinse and repeat. How often you wish to repeat this simple process is up to you, the recipe you have made, as well as with that of your particular goal or need.

This entire process usually takes about 10 to 15 minutes and is an enjoyable and relaxing activity.

Finally, remember that to get the results you desire you must also do your part by taking the appropriate inspired actions necessary toward achieving your goal or intention.

When it comes to utilizing the Law of Attraction in your life, taking action is like hinges on the door of manifestation. Listen to your intuition, ask your spiritual team what the next best course of action is to obtain your particular goal, and more importantly go do it! No action, no results. Period.

How to Energetically Empower Your Recipes

With herbal medicine, especially in the field of Chinese herbalism, practitioners amplify the power within herbs and plants in order to magnify the energies needed to create their desired intention for healing. This also holds true with herbal folklore.

In themselves, the healing properties of herbs on the mind, body, and soul are quite powerful. But you can magnify their intensity with your own bioenergy. Combining your own bioenergy, or chi as it is known in Oriental medicine, will make the recipes in this book truly effective.

Plants and herbs have been known to possess certain energetic qualities useful for specific needs. Roses draw love, peppermint draws money, Eucalyptus heals, and Gardenia increases psychic awareness.

Many plants and herbs contain several useful energetic properties such as cinnamon, which can be used to promote healing, love, money, protection, psychic awareness, and spirituality.

Just as with that of herbs and plants, the archangels also have specific functions and energetic qualities assigned to them. Archangel Michael, for example, is known for the energetic qualities of protection, courage, and life purpose.

Combining the unique energy vibrations of the archangels with the energies of plants and herbs corresponding to your goal or intention, as well as that of your own life force energy, is one of the fastest ways to manifest love, healing, abundance, money, etc.

Basic Functions and Energetic Qualities of the Archangels

Note: a detailed description of the energetic qualities of the archangels along with the plants and herbs that correspond with their energy frequencies can be found in the appendix of this book.

Archangel Michael

Protection – Spiritual Protection – Cutting Cords – Life purpose Guidance – Clearing and Shielding – Personal Power – Clearing Ego and Fear – Clearing Lower Energies

Archangel Raphael

Healing of People and Animals – Healing Wisdom

Archangel Gabriel

Angel of Teaching – Creative Writing – Art – Channeling - Communication – Child Adoption – Child Conception and Fertility

Archangel Uriel

Intellectual Understanding – Ideas – Insights – Creativity – Unconditional Forgiveness

Archangel Chamuel

The Finding Angel – Relationship Healing – Finding Love – Finding Lost Objects – Finding a New Job – Finding a New House – Discovering New Wisdom

Archangel Ariel

Angel of Nature, Animals and Nature Spirits – Manifestation – Environmentalism

Archangel Metatron

Esoteric Healing Work – Universal Energies – Time Management – Organizational Skill – Spiritual Growth

Archangel Sandalphon

Life Guidance – Music – Mercy – Prayer – Grounding

Archangel Azrael

Releasing Grief – Emotional Healing - Mediumship

Archangel Jophiel

Love - Positive Thinking and Feeling – Clearing Subconscious Clutter – Beauty

Archangel Haniel

Awakening – Intuition – Clairvoyance – Releasing old patterns

Archangel Raziel

Remembering and Healing Past Lives – Esoteric Wisdom – Dream Interpretation

Archangel Raguel

Healing Arguments and Misunderstandings – Bringing Harmony to Relationships – Fairness in Legal Issues

Archangel Jeremiel

Spiritual Vision – Life Review

Archangel Zadkiel

Healing Painful Memories – Divine Mission – Spiritual Gifts

Blessing and Charging Your Recipes

Plants and herbs can be programmed to amplify the energetic resonance of your goals and intentions, combined with the energy of each specific Archangel. This process is known as blessing or charging your recipe.

When blessing or charging my recipes I often will light a candle, and play some soothing music in the background, but this is optional.

You do not need to perform any special ritual when energetically charging your recipes, but you do need a basic understanding of how to feel and build up life force energy in your hands.

Energy healers are very skilled at doing this. The good news is that it is an easy skill to learn.

How to Feel the Life Force Energy in Your Hands

1.   Rub Your Hands Together Briskly for about 30 Seconds.

2.   Place your palms in front of you, facing each other at a distance of about 4 inches apart.

3.   Slowly, push your palms towards one another (do not touch the palms together), and then slowly pull them back out, almost as if you're playing an invisible accordion. Do this for about 1 to 2 minutes and simply notice any sensations in your hands.

4.   As you continue to do this you will begin to notice various sensations between your palms.

Pay attention to any sensations in your hands such as heat, vibrating, tingling, or a slight resistance like that of a magnetic repulsion. These are signs that you have activated and have gathered life force energy or chi.

The Empowering Rite

A corresponding prayer, such as those shared in this book are not necessary but adds another effective energetic component. If you are going to use one of these prayers, you would read it aloud prior to activating the energy between your hands.

To bless and charge your finished recipe place your energetically activated hands around the jar, bottle, or other container housing your ingredients. Feel the vital energy inside your hands as you imagine brilliant white light emanating from your palms infusing the ingredients.

As you do this repeat the following *Simple Prayer of Blessing*:

"I now charge this recipe with Love and Light! Thank you, God and the Archangels for blessing these ingredients with the highest and best intention for all concerned. And so it is, Amen!"

Keep your activated hands around your recipe and begin to visualize the end result of your intention or goal corresponding with your recipe as if it already happened, feeling the gratitude, joy, relief, happiness, or any other related emotion that comes up for you.

Stay in this place of reverie for a minimum of ten minutes. I generally select a piece of music that will play for this length of time, but you may also set a timer if you wish.

After practice, you will find that you no longer need to time yourself as the energy inside your hands will "turn off" signaling that you are done.

When you are finished thank God and the Angels for their assistance.

The Angelic Pantry; Basic Ingredients

This chapter will list some of the basic plants, herbs, and oils used in the recipes found in this book.

It is intended to introduce you to the most common plants, herbs, and oils used in this book, along with their resonating properties. More importantly, the plants, herbs, and oils suggested in this book are easy to find, inexpensive, and many can be found at your local grocery, and will also provide you with a well-stocked pantry for all of your energetic workings with the archangels.

The Basic 50 Herbs and Plants & Their Energetic Properties

Allspice – Money; luck; healing.

Anise – Protection; purification; intuition; luck. Use for protection, meditation, and intuition-enhancing incenses.

Angelica – Protection; purification; cleansing auric field. Angelica protects by both creating a barrier against negative energy, and by filling its user with positive energy.

Basil - Love; money; protection. Best known for its properties to aid and strengthen love, and to also bring about prosperity.

Bay - Healing; protection; purification; intuition.

Bergamot Mint - Money; success; prosperity; abundance.

Catnip – Happiness, love; beauty; meditation; enhancing intuition.

Cedar - Purification; health and healing; luck; good fortune; happiness; exorcism; money and prosperity; justice; protection; harmony; meditation; peace.

Chamomile - Love; money; purification; meditation; harmony.

Cinnamon – Meditation; protection; energy; creativity; divination; success; money; healing; love; lucid dreaming.

Clove - Success; wealth; prosperity; protection; healing; creativity; divination; getting rid of negative thoughts.

Coriander – Love; healing; repairing relationships.

Dandelion – Enhancing intuition; divination; angelic communication. Both root and flowers are used.

Dill – Money; love; protection.

Fennel – Health; healing; protection; purification.

Frankincense – Part used – resin. Burn for protection, exorcism, spirituality, love, consecration, blessing, energy, strength, visions, healing, meditation, power and courage.

Gardenia – Love; peace; health; healing; spirituality; enhancing intuition.

Heather – Spirituality; angelic communication; love; luck; peace; protection.

Honeysuckle – Prosperity; health and healing; love; creativity; prophetic dreams; protection; enhancing intuitive awareness; divination; clairvoyance.

Jasmine – Love; spirituality; money; prophetic dreams.

Juniper – Protection; purification; healing; love.

Lavender – Creativity; happiness; love; harmony; abundance; prosperity; enhancing intuition; success; purification; protection.

Lemon – Purification; healing; love. Parts used – dried peel or fruit.

Lemongrass – Purification; spirituality; enhancing intuition.

Lilac – Creativity; clairvoyance; enhancing intuition; divination; happiness; peace; spirituality; protection; exorcism.

Marigold – Love; respect; relationship harmony; equitable court decisions; protection.

Magnolia – Love; beauty; relationship harmony; health; peace; emotional balance.

Marjoram – Love; abundance; happiness; purification; protection; cleansing.

Mugwort – Enhancing intuition; lucid dreaming; prophetic dreams.

Myrrh – Healing; purification; spirituality; purification; meditation.

Nutmeg – Prosperity and abundance; divination; enhancing intuition; justice; clairvoyance; spirituality; meditation.

Orange – Love; prosperity; purification; healing; divination; balance; harmony; enhancing intuition.

Oregano – Happiness; harmony; protection; grief; prosperity; love; peace; enhancing intuition.

Parsley – Joy; happiness; divination; clairvoyance; cleansing; purification; enhancing intuition.

Patchouli – Prosperity; protection; love; fertility; purification.

Peppermint – Health; healing; love; money; purification; exorcism; enhancing intuition.

Pine – Cleansing; consecration; divination; happiness; healing; love; money; passion; prosperity; protection; psychic development; purification; grief.

Rose – Love; spirituality; friendship; domestic peace/happiness; lasting relationship.

Rosemary – All-purpose herb. Love; money; spirituality; protection; success; prosperity; abundance. Can be substituted for any herbs.

Sage – Exorcism; protection; purification; wisdom; health; healing; money; spirituality

St. John's Wort – Healing; protection; purification.
Sandalwood – Protection; healing; exorcism; spirituality; meditation; manifestation.

Spearmint – Healing; love; protection while sleeping.

Tarragon – Love; peace; meditation.

Thyme – Clairvoyance; enhancing intuition; purification; courage; divination; lucid dreams, exorcism; happiness; healing; love; money, prevents nightmares; protection; grieving; meditation.

Vanilla – Love; money; energy; mental stimulation; creativity. Parts used the pod, beans, and pure extract.

Violet – Protection; love; peace; spirituality; manifesting; meditation.

Yarrow – Protection; divination; love; relationship happiness; enhancing intuition; clairvoyance; purification.

Essential Oils by Name & Associated Energetic Properties

Allspice - Prosperity; courage; energy; healing.

Anise/Star Anise - Purification; protection.

Basil Sweet - Love; money; protection; mental clarity.

Bergamot Mint - Money; success; abundance.

Carnation – Protection; healing; strength; love.

Cedar – Purification; healing; money; exorcism.

Cinnamon – Money; prosperity; success; healing; love; healing.

Clove – Success; wealth; prosperity; protection; healing; creativity.

Eucalyptus – Purification; healing; protection.

Frankincense - Spirituality; protection; consecration; exorcism.

Gardenia – Love; peace; happiness; healing.

Ginger – Prosperity; abundance; love; energy.

Hibiscus – Love; spirituality; intuition.

Honeysuckle – Money; spirituality; intuition; friendship; happiness; healing.

Jasmine – Love; money; wisdom; lucid dreaming.

Juniper – Protection; peace; exorcism.

Lavender – Love; happiness; purification; healing.

Lemon – Healing; love; purification.

Lemongrass – mental clarity; wisdom; intuition.

Lilac – Protection; spirituality.

Magnolia – Spirituality; meditation; balance.

Musk – Love; prosperity; purification; wisdom; spirituality.

Myrrh – Purification; meditation; healing; spirituality; exorcism.

Neroli – Confidence; love; lucid dreaming.

Orange – Love; money; intuition; lucid dreaming.

Patchouli – Love; protection; purification.

Peppermint – Money; energy; creativity.

Pine – Grounding; healing; energy.

Rose – Love; spirituality; meditation; friendship; healing; fertility; abundance.

Rose Geranium – Confidence; self-love; grounding; rebalancing; emotional healing.

Rosemary – All purpose. Love; money; spirituality; protection; success; prosperity; abundance.

Sage – Protection; cleansing; spirituality; wisdom; exorcism.

Sandalwood – Spirituality; protection; healing; lucid dreaming; exorcism.

Vanilla – Love; spirituality; intuition; mental clarity.

Violet - Wisdom; luck; love; protection; healing.

Yarrow – Courage; intuition; protection.

Ylang-ylang – Harmony; love; spirituality; meditation; happiness.

Notes:

Incense

Incense has been used in spiritual rites for thousands of years. Many spiritual traditions believed that burning incense carried prayers to the gods and goddesses. It was also believed that incense created a sacred space for these deities to manifest.

In modern times, many of these beliefs still hold true and incense has been used to bless, purify, shield and protect, exorcize, raise consciousness, as well as to set the tone for worship and devotion.

The use of incense is also symbolic of the transformations you desire. Each herb or plant burned has its own unique energy signature which corresponds to a certain goal or need.

When the incense is either heated or smoldered these unique energy signatures are released; mixing with your own personal vibration and intent, activating the Law of Attraction.

When combined with the energy signatures of the archangels the result is a speedy manifestation of your heartfelt prayers and desires.

Basic Forms of Incense

There are two basic forms of incense: combustible, the type you burn or smolder (such as incense cones and sticks) and noncombustible incense, that has been ground into a powder form and either sprinkled on to incense charcoal to burn, or alternatively placed on it and essential oil burner with a small amount of oil, and then heated to release their unique aromas.

The recipes shared in this chapter are of the noncombustible variety simply because they do not produce much smoke (or none at all if you are using and essential oil burner) when you heat them.

Also, loose herbal incense is easy to make as well as inexpensive.

Burning Herbs Vs Heating Them

The aroma of the herbal incense recipes will be different should you burn them versus heating them using an essential oil burner. Which method you choose to use as a matter of preference.

I personally use both methods, and when burning the herbs I prefer simpler one ingredient dried herbs that correspond with my intent, such as a sage leaf or a dried Rosemary sprig.

Loose dried herbs can also be used to coat lightly oiled candles of all sizes. To do this, sprinkle the powdered herbal incense mixture onto a paper towel. Next, roll the oil candle in the mixture. The herbal incense does not have to coat the entire candle to be effective.

Caution: never leave incense burning or heating unattended! And always keep them out of reach from children and pets.

Supplies You Need to Burn Loose Herbs

To burn loose herbs you will need and incense censer specifically designed to hold a small disc of incense charcoal. Once the incense charcoal is lit and placed in the censer it will be hot. I recommend putting the incense censer on a dish or in bowl filled with sand first.

Should you need to move the censer after you light the charcoal disc it will be easier to handle.

Incense censers and charcoal discs can be found online at various metaphysical bookstores, and at many Catholic gift shops. Amazon.com also has a great selection with high-quality craftsmanship, and more importantly at bargain prices.

Tips for Using This Method

Use loose herbal incense sparingly. Only sprinkle a half teaspoonful of herbs on the charcoal disc at a time. Do not overload the censer. When the smoke stops that is your signal to add more of your chosen herbal incense recipe.

Supplies You Need to Heat Loose Herbs

To heat loose herbs you will need and aromatherapy oil burner, also known as an essential oil burner, and about 2 teaspoons of natural oil such as extra-virgin olive oil (my favorite) almond oil, or vegetable oil.

Add the oil in the bowl or base of the oil burner first and then sprinkle about 1 teaspoon of herbal incense in the oil, light the tea candle, and you're done! I really enjoy this method. The aroma released from the incense is always bright and refreshing, as well as smoke-free.

As an added bonus with this method, you can even use fresh herbs. Just make sure you chop them up finely or crush a small amount in your mortar and pestle prior to using them. This will help to release their natural oils when they are placed in the warm oil.

Basic Supplies Needed to Create Herbal Incense Recipes

- Jars or containers to store your herbal incense blends
- A mortar and pestle
- Measuring spoons
- Cutting board or other working space

The basic supplies for making your herbal incense recipes are minimal, and each supply is easy to find and purchase.

The mortar and pestle are used to grind larger herbs and plants into a powder, as well as to release and to combine their essences.

Incense Recipes

A "part" is any unit of measurement you wish to use, provided that it's consistent throughout the entire recipe. For example, a "part" can be equal amounts in teaspoons, tablespoons, and cups.

I generally use tablespoon measurements because I like to make smaller batches of loose herbal incense, but feel free to use a unit of measurement you most prefer as long as it is uniform throughout the recipe.

Basic Angelic Altar Incense

1 part cinnamon
2 parts myrrh
3 parts frankincense

A general altar incense and room purifier.

Archangel Ariel Basic Incense

1 part cedar
1 part Juniper
2 parts frankincense

Corresponds with all the attributes of Archangel Ariel.

Archangel Azrael Basic Incense

1 part benzoin
1 part frankincense
1 part myrrh

Corresponds with all the attributes of Archangel Azrael.

Archangel Chamuel Basic Incense

2 parts benzoin

2 parts sandalwood
a few drops rose oil

Corresponds with all the attributes of Archangel Chamuel.

Archangel Gabriel Basic Incense

1 part nutmeg
2 parts benzoin
2 parts frankincense

Corresponds with all the attributes of Archangel Gabriel.

Archangel Haniel Basic Incense

1 part lemon peel
1 part rose petals
2 parts gardenia petals
2 parts myrrh
a few drops jasmine oil

Corresponds with all the attributes of Archangel Haniel.

Archangel Jeremiel Basic Incense

1 part ginger
1 part pine

2 parts frankincense
Corresponds with all the attributes of Archangel Jeremiel.

Archangel Metatron Basic Incense

1 part cypress
2 parts nutmeg
a few drops patchouli oil

Corresponds with all the attributes of Archangel Metatron.

Archangel Michael Basic Incense

1 part orange
2 parts sandalwood
3 parts frankincense
one pinch saffron

Corresponds with all the attributes of Archangel Michael.

Archangel Raguel Basic Incense

1 part nutmeg
1 part myrrh
2 parts frankincense

Corresponds with all the attributes of Archangel Raguel.

Archangel Raphael Basic Incense

½ part cinnamon
1 part myrrh
2 parts frankincense

Corresponds with all the attributes of Archangel Raphael.

Archangel Raziel Basic Incense

1 part Juniper berries
1 part sandalwood
2 parts frankincense

Corresponds with all the attributes of Archangel Raziel.

Archangel Sandalphon Basic Incense

1 part lemon peel
1 part lavender
2 parts frankincense

Corresponds with all the attributes of Archangel Sandalphon.

Archangel Uriel Basic Incense

1 part cypress
1 part sandalwood
1 part pine

Corresponds with all the attributes of Archangel Uriel.

Archangel Zadkiel Basic Incense

1/2 part lemon
1/2 part orange
2 parts frankincense

Corresponds with all the attributes of Archangel Zadkiel.

Archangel Jophiel I Love You Incense Powder

1 part anise powder
1 part patchouli powder
1 part ground dried orange peel
3 parts dried rose petals
tea light candles

To enhance love in all of its many forms, sprinkle on top of a tea light candle and burn candle in an area where it will not be disturbed by children or pets.

Archangel Michael Space Purifying Incense

1 part lavender
1 part rosemary
1 part white sage

Use to purify your living space from negative energies.

Archangel Raphael Speedy Recovery Incense

1 part Sweetgrass
1 part pine needles
2 parts Juniper berries
2 parts frankincense

Burn to encourage the speedy recovery of your body, mind, and spirit.

Archangel Raziel Epiphany Incense

1 part myrrh
1 part Tonka beans
2 parts cedar
2 parts patchouli

Use to encourage God-given ideas, inspirations, and solutions.

Archangel Haniel Creative Inspiration Incense

1 part cinnamon
1 part anise
1 part ginger
2 parts cedar
2 parts frankincense

Use for creative inspiration and to heighten to your intuition.

Archangel Haniel Happy Heart Incense

1/2 part lavender
1 part cinnamon
1 part marjoram
3 parts lemon balm

Use to lift your personal vibration with joy and happiness.

Archangel Raguel Harmonious Spirit Incense

1/2 part lavender
1 part orange
3 parts cedar

Use to restore harmony in relationships.

Archangel Jophiel Blossoming Love Incense

1/2 part orange peel
1 part lemon balm
2 parts mastic

Use to strengthen the bonds of a blossoming new love.

Archangel Jophiel Soulmate Incense

1/2 part orris root
2 parts rose petals
3 parts sandalwood

Use to deepen your bond with your soul other.

Archangel Haniel Meditative Awareness Incense

1 part cinnamon
1 part clove
2 parts cedar wood
4 parts sandalwood

A sweet, meditative incense with a slight spicy accent.

Archangel Sandalphon Heavens Praise Incense

1 part lavender
1 part lemon balm
2 parts frankincense

Great to use while offering up prayers of thanksgiving and songs of praise.

Archangel Raziel Healing Hands Incense

1 part frankincense
1 part mastic
1 part myrrh

Great for use while performing healing work of any kind, as well as while praying for healing for yourself or loved one.

Archangel Michael Serene Forest Incense

1 part calamus
1 part oak moss
3 parts aloes wood

Use to release stress and anxiety caused by negative thinking, or while meditating or studying.

Archangel Metatron Meditative Bliss Incense

1/2 part lavender
1/2 part marjoram
3 parts sandalwood

To promote a relaxing, meditative environment for spiritual awareness and inner growth.

Archangel Jophiel Sensuous Elegance Incense

1/4 part orange peel
1 part rose petals
2 parts sandalwood

Use to set a sensuous and romantic mood. As my spirit friend David likes to say, "Hubba, hubba, hubba!"

Archangel Gabriel Fertility Incense

1/2 part cinnamon
1/2 part nutmeg
1 part patchouli
2 parts cedar
4 parts sandalwood

A relaxing blend to use when trying to conceive a child. Also works well when birthing new, artistic ideas.

Archangel Azrael Peaceful Sleep Incense

1 part benzoin
1 part frankincense
1 part valerian
4 parts myrrh

Use to relax the mind and body for a deep, restful night sleep.

Archangel Raziel Lucid Dreams Incense

1 part bay
1 part rose petals
2 parts sage

Use prior to sleep to stimulate lucid dreaming

Archangel Ariel Enriched Prosperity Incense

1 part benzoin
1 part cinnamon
1 part nutmeg
1 part ginger
6 parts calamus

Use to bring more abundance and prosperity in your life.

Archangel Michael Shield of Courage Incense

1 part cinnamon
1 part cloves
1 part cumin
3 parts aloes wood
3 parts sandalwood

Use to dispel fear, bolster your courage, as well as to surround yourself and your living space with Archangel Michaels protective shield of courage.

Archangel Haniel Psychic Awareness Incense

1 part rosemary
1 part orange
3 parts sandalwood

Use to sharpen your psychic awareness.

Notes:

Essential Oils

Essential oils were mankind's first medicine. Egyptian hieroglyphics and ancient Chinese manuscripts reveal that priests and physicians have been using essential oils for thousands of years.

There are over 188 references of essential oils used in the Holy Bible. Oils such as rosemary, hyssop, spikenard, frankincense, and myrrh were used for anointing and healing the sick. In the book of Exodus God gave Moses a recipe for a 'holy anointing oil' containing olive oil, myrrh, sweet cinnamon, and other herbs.

In the New Testament, there are several accounts of the use of essential oils for healing and anointing.

How Do Essential Oils Work?

In modern times, essential oils have been found to not only affect the physical body but also help to balance your emotions as well. Numerous scientific studies have revealed that inhaling certain essential oils and oil combinations stimulate the olfactory bulb through the nasal cavity. The olfactory bulb is connected to a part of the brain called the limbic system which is responsible for physical, mental, and emotional health.

When applied topically to the skin, the properties of essential oils are absorbed into the bloodstream, dispersing to the specific organs and systems on which they work.

Metaphysically the use of essential oils raises your overall energetic vibration not only activating the Law of Attraction but your connection to God and the Angels as well.

Using Essential Oils

The use of essential oils is very versatile. Essential oils can be used to anoint the chakra points, worn as a perfume, put into bath water, used to anoint candles, placed in an aromatherapy diffuser or an essential oil burner, or used in hydrosols and sprays.

One word of caution - never apply undiluted essential oils to your skin. Essential oils are highly concentrated and can contain certain oils that can burn your skin. Always test a small amount on the inside of your wrist first. Undiluted use of essential oils on the skin can cause irritation or an allergic reaction in some people. Above all never use essential oils on broken skin, and *never ingest them*.

To dilute essential oils, use a carrier oil such as extra-virgin olive oil, jojoba oil, or other similar organic vegetable oil.

Also, and this applies to the other recipes in this book as well, *always check with your medical doctor prior to using essential oils; especially if you're pregnant or nursing.*

Where to Buy Essential Oils

Essential oils can be purchased from health food stores, and there are plenty of options to purchase them online as well.

To keep their unique energy signatures at a maximum I suggest pure, organic essential oils as opposed to synthetic. Many people are allergic to synthetic compounds. Read the label thoroughly before purchasing your essential oils.

Basic Supplies

Basic supplies for making essential oil blends are minimal:

- A natural carrier oil of your choice such as extra-virgin olive oil, jojoba, almond, safflower, or other similar organic vegetable oil
- An eyedropper should the essential oil bottle not include a single drop dispenser
- Airtight, opaque or dark-colored glass bottles, jars, or containers. For the following recipes in this chapter 1-

ounce (30 ml) glass bottles work the best and can be purchased online.

Always store your essential oil bottles in a cool, dark place. Use within 3 to 4 months as many of these oil blends will go rancid.

Essential Oil Recipes

Archangel Michael Essential Oil Recipe

2 drops orange essential oil
2 drops rosemary essential oil
4 drops sandalwood essential oil
8 drops frankincense essential oil
1/8 cup extra virgin olive oil

Use for guidance, direction, and clarity. Rub a few drops on a candle, or on a quartz crystal while praying to Archangel Michael for clarity of purpose.

Archangel Metatron Essential Oil Recipe

2 drops sandalwood essential oil
6 drops myrrh essential oil
8 drops frankincense essential oil
1/8 cup extra virgin olive oil

1-ounce glass bottle

Use for spiritual cleansing and purification. Rub a few drops onto your wrist pulse points while asking to Archangel Metatron to shield you from any negative energies due to current planetary shifts, or rub a few drops on to a candle prior to burning.

Archangel Michael Room Purification Spray

6 drops lavender essential oil
9 drops lemon essential oil
15 drops Clary Sage essential oil
3 ounces distilled water
4-ounce glass spray bottle

Fill the bottle with distilled water and essential oils. Do not overfill bottle with water so that the ingredients can mix well. Shake well before using. Spray around the room or other space to remove negative energies in the area replacing them with the energies of peace and love.

Archangel Azrael Hallows Eve Oil

6 drops cinnamon essential oil
6 drops ginger essential oil
4 drops nutmeg essential oil
2 drops clove essential oil

1/8 cup extra virgin olive oil

To protect against spirit tricksters on Halloween night, or to honor your loved ones or pets in heaven, place 4 to 6 drops in 1/2 cup of boiling water allowing the fragrance to fill the room (do not drink). Smells like pumpkin pie!

Archangel Gabriel Winter Solstice Oil

4 drops cedar essential oil
4 drops orange essential oil
4 drops Juniper essential oil
8 drops pine essential oil
1/8 cup extra virgin olive oil

To evoke the scents of the winter holiday season, use a few drops to anoint a candle, or place a few drops on an aromatherapy burner. You can also add a few drops onto a cinnamon stick and use as simple potpourri.

Archangel Raphael Immune Support Spray

10 drops lavender essential oil
10 drops bergamot essential oil
4 drops lemon essential oil
4 drops tea tree oil
3 ounces distilled water
4-ounce glass spray bottle

Fill bottle with distilled water and essential oils. Do not overfill bottle so ingredients can mix well. Shake well before using. Spray around the room, or into your hands to boost your immune system. Great use before entering public places. Do not spray on face.

Archangel Gabriel Christmas Spirit Mist

4 drops rosemary essential oil
6 drops cinnamon essential oil
6 drops orange essential oil
6 drops frankincense essential oil
3 ounces distilled water
4-ounce glass spray bottle

Fill bottle with distilled water and essential oils. Do not overfill bottle so ingredients can mix well. Shake well before using. Spray around the room to invoke the Christmas spirit. Great to use while decorating the Christmas tree. Do not spray on face.

Archangel Gazardiel New Year Blessing Oil

10 drops bergamot essential oil
5 drops of grapefruit essential oil
5 drops Cypress essential oil
5 drops frankincense essential oil
2 drops jasmine essential oil

1 drop ginger essential oil
1/8 cup extra virgin olive oil

Mix all ingredients well. To bless your intentions for the New Year, rub a few drops on your wrists or heart chakra while feeling gratitude as if you've already achieved what it is you desire.

Archangel Jeremiel Envision Essential Oil

8 drops geranium essential oil
5 drops rose essential oil
3 drops orange essential oil
2 drops lavender essential oil
2 drops spruce essential oil
2 drops Sage essential oil
1/8 cup extra virgin olive oil

Mix all ingredients well. To awaken and inspire your dreams and to expel negative emotions and emotional blocks, rub a few drops on your wrist pulse points or throat chakra.

Archangel Chamuel Romantic Rose Mist

4 drops bergamot essential oil
4 drops patchouli essential oil
6 drops ylang-ylang essential oil
12 drops rose essential oil

3 ounces distilled water
4-ounce glass spray bottle

Fill bottle with distilled water and essential oils. Do not overfill bottle so ingredients can mix well. Shake well before using. Spray on pillows and sheets to inspire romance. Do not spray on face.

Archangel Michael Aura Clearing Oil Blend

4 drops ylang-ylang essential oil
8 drops lavender essential oil
16 drops orange essential oil
1/8 cup extra virgin olive oil

Mix all ingredients well. To quickly clear your outer auric layer, rub a few drops onto your pulse points while asking Archangel Michael to cleanse and clear your bioenergetic body. Also great for energetic pickup!

Archangel Jeremiel Mental Clarity Essential Oil

4 drops geranium essential oil
4 drops peppermint essential oil
10 drops rosemary essential oil
1/8 cup extra virgin olive oil

Mix all ingredients well. To soothe racing thoughts and to promote mental clarity and alertness, inhale the aromatic vapors directly from the container, or place a few drops in an essential oil burner or diffuser to fill a room with its scent.

Archangel Haniel Happy Heart Essential Oil

8 drops lavender essential oil
12 drops rose or rose geranium essential oil
1/8 cup extra virgin olive oil

Mix all ingredients well. To promote love and a happy heart rub a few drops onto your wrist pulse points or heart chakra or add several drops undiluted in an essential oil burner. The fragrance is absolutely heavenly!

Archangel Zadkiel Happiness Diffuser Blend

2 drops geranium essential oil
3 drops bergamot essential oil
3 drops lavender essential oil
aromatherapy diffuser

Add oils into your aromatherapy diffuser according to manufacturer instructions. Use to create a mood of joy and happiness in your living space. Great to use when you're having people over and are ready to entertain.

Archangel Raphael Emotional Support Diffuser Blend

2 drops orange essential oil
2 drops bergamot essential oil
2 drops Cypress essential oil
2 drops frankincense essential oil
aromatherapy diffuser

Add oils into your aromatherapy diffuser according to manufacturer instructions. Use to ease emotional sadness and heartbreak as a result of a relationship breakup, or death of a loved one or pet. This blend is very soothing and comforting to the senses.

Archangel Jophiel Summertime Room Spritzer

3 drops cinnamon essential oil
5 drops jasmine essential oil
5 drops clove essential oil
6 drops orange essential oil
3 ounces distilled water
4-ounce glass spray bottle

Fill bottle with distilled water and essential oils. Do not overfill bottle with water so ingredients can mix well. Shake well before using. Use to fill the room with the nostalgic fragrance of summer. Also, doubles as an insect repellent!

Archangel Gabriel Back to School Oil Blend

8 drops bergamot essential oil
8 drops marjoram essential oil
10 drops lavender essential oil
10 drops lemon essential oil
1/8 cup extra virgin olive oil

Mix all ingredients well in store in a glass container or jar. To relieve stress from the new back-to-school routine rub a few drops on your pulse points, or place a few drops on a cotton ball and inhale the fresh aroma.

Archangel Azrael Sweet Summer Dreams Oil

8 drops Roman chamomile essential oil
8 drops orange essential oil
2 drops honeysuckle essential oil
1/8 cup extra virgin olive oil

Mix all ingredients well. Store in a glass bottle. For a relaxing and refreshing night's sleep apply to pulse points prior to retiring. Especially good after a hectic day of sightseeing!

Archangel Jophiel Creativity Oil Blend

4 drops sandalwood essential oil
8 drops vanilla essential oil
20 drops cinnamon essential oil
20 drops clove essential oil
20 drops bergamot essential oil
30 drops sweet orange essential oil

Mix all ingredients well. Store in a glass bottle. Place a few drops in your aromatherapy burner or diffuser, or place a few drops on a cotton ball in place in your creative working space. Use to boost your creative muse. Fabulous for use while writing, painting, drawing, or any other creative endeavor.

Archangel Uriel Concentration Diffuser Blend

2 drops rosemary essential oil
6 drops basil essential oil
20 drops lemon essential oil
aromatherapy diffuser

Add oils to your diffuser according to manufacturer instructions. Use to sharpen your concentration and boost your productivity. Great to use while studying or for work activities that require your full attention.

Archangel Raphael Heal the Sick Oil Blend

8 drops cinnamon essential oil
8 drops clove essential oil
8 drops eucalyptus essential oil
8 drops lemon essential oil
8 drops rosemary essential oil
1/8 cup extra virgin olive oil

Mix all ingredients well in store in a glass container. This is the angelic version of the popular 'Five Thieves Oil' healing recipe. This blend has antiviral, and antifungal properties. To use, apply 3 to 4 drops topically to the bottom of the feet, throat, and behind the ears. _Caution!_ Always wear socks after applying this mixture, and avoid going into the shower or other wet area for a few hours as the oil will cause the bottom of your feet to be slippery.

Archangel Raphael Heal the Sick Room Mist

8 drops cinnamon essential oil
8 drops clove essential oil
8 drops eucalyptus essential oil
8 drops lemon essential oil
8 drops rosemary essential oil
3 ounces distilled water
4-ounce glass spray bottle

Fill bottle with distilled water and essential oils. Do not overfill bottle with water so ingredients can mix well. Shake well before using. Use to cleanse and disinfect your living space from germs, especially when someone in your house is sick. This is also great to spray on your hands before and after entering a public place.

Archangel Raziel Success Oil Blend ⚹

3 drops basil essential oil
3 drops cinnamon essential oil
3 drops patchouli essential oil
12 drops bergamot essential oil
1/8 cup extra virgin olive oil

Mix all ingredients well and store in a glass container. Use a few drops to anoint a candle, or place a 10 to 15 undiluted drops on an aromatherapy burner while visualizing or affirming success.

Archangel Raphael Energy Oil Blend

2 drops patchouli essential oil
4 drops grapefruit essential oil
4 drops lime essential oil
8 drops sweet orange essential oil
1/8 cup extra virgin olive oil

Mix all ingredients well and store in a glass container. For an additional burst of energy apply a few drops to your pulse points, or place 10 to 15 drops undiluted in an aromatherapy burner.

Archangel Haniel Productivity Oil Blend

2 drops Roman chamomile essential oil
2 drops lime essential oil
4 drops lemon essential oil
4 drops lemongrass essential oil
6 drops sweet orange essential oil
1/8 cup extra virgin olive oil

Mix all ingredients well. Store in a glass container. To supercharge your productivity, apply a few drops on a cotton ball and placing your working space, or place 10 to 15 drops undiluted in an aromatherapy burner.

Archangel Chamuel New Job Oil Blend

4 drops cardamom essential oil
4 drops clove essential oil
12 drops ginger essential oil
1/8 cup extra virgin olive oil

Mix all ingredients well, and store in a glass container. Looking for new job? Apply a few drops to a cotton ball and keep near you while job searching, or place 10 to 15 drops undiluted in an aromatherapy burner.

Archangel Jophiel Love Potion No. 8

4 drops cinnamon essential oil
10 drops patchouli essential oil
10 drops vanilla essential oil
1/8 cup extra virgin olive oil

Mix all ingredients well, and store in a glass container. To use apply a few drops on your wrist and neck pulse points. The fragrance of this oil blend is subtle yet sexy!

Archangel Haniel Goodbye Anger Diffusing Oil

5 drops jasmine essential oil
5 drops ylang-ylang essential oil
10 drops bergamot essential oil
aromatherapy diffuser

Add oils to your diffuser according to manufacturer instructions. Use to balance yourself mentally, emotionally, and spiritually after an encounter that causes you anger. This diffusing oil blend is sure to help you to regain your bliss! Also great to use on those occasional evenings when the kids seem to be acting out.

Archangel Gabriel Energize Me Diffusing Oil

8 drops bergamot essential oil
12 drops grapefruit essential oil
aromatherapy diffuser

Add oils to your diffuser according to manufacturer instructions. Use whenever you need to energize yourself physically and mentally. This diffusing oil blend is also spectacular to use during creative writing projects or journaling.

Archangel Jophiel Never Alone Diffuser Blend

2 drops rose geranium essential oil
6 drops Roman chamomile essential oil
12 drops bergamot essential oil
aromatherapy diffuser

Add oils to your diffuser according to manufacturer instructions. Use whenever you feel lonely. This diffusing oil blend is fragrant and comforting and serves as a great reminder that you're Guardian Angels are surrounding you 24 x 7.

Archangel Michael Monsters Be Gone Mist

8 drops lemon essential oil
12 drops rose geranium essential oil
3 ounces distilled water
4-ounce glass spray bottle

Fill bottle with distilled water and essential oils. Do not overfill bottle with water so ingredients can mix well. Shake well before using. Use to calm your child's fears and anxieties about monsters, ghosts, zombies, and the boogie man. Spray in closets, under the bed, and around the room reminding your child that Archangel Michael is protecting them with his sword of brilliant, blue light.

Archangel Zadkiel Tension Eraser Diffuser Blend

4 drops ylang-ylang essential oil
8 drops Roman chamomile essential oil
8 drops sandalwood essential oil
aromatherapy diffuser

Add oils to your diffuser according to manufacturer instructions. Use to melt away relationship tension. Also fabulous to use during family gatherings, reunions, and holidays.

Archangel Sandalphon Peace Be Still Oil Diffuser Blend

15 drops Roman chamomile essential oil
15 drops lavender essential oil
aromatherapy diffuser

Ad oils to your diffuser according to manufacturer instructions. Use to dispel fearful thoughts, and to create an environment of peace and serenity.

Archangel Raphael Perk Me Up Mist

4 drops frankincense essential oil
8 drops grapefruit essential oil
8 drops peppermint essential oil
3 ounces distilled water
4-ounce glass spray bottle

Fill bottle with distilled water and essential oils. Do not overfill bottle with water so ingredients can mix well. Shake well before using. Spray around your home or work environment for instant mental alertness and clarity. A perfect pick me up on those days when you need an added energetic boost.

Archangel Raziel General Blessing Oil Blend

2 drops ginger essential oil
2 drops ylang-ylang essential oil
4 drops cedarwood essential oil
4 drops frankincense essential oil
4 drops lemon essential oil
8 drops bergamot essential oil
1/8 cup extra virgin olive oil

Mix all ingredients well, and store in a glass container. To bless your desires and bring them into fruition quicker, apply a few drops to a candle, quartz crystal, or place 10 to 15 drops undiluted in an aromatherapy burner.

Prayer Oils

The following are general purpose prayer oils. Mix all ingredients well and store in a one-ounce glass bottle. Use a few drops to anoint a candle before praying, or add a few drops to your aromatherapy burner.

Note: The prayer oil recipes below use organic, extra virgin olive oil as the carrier oil, but please feel free to substitute almond, coconut, or jojoba oil.

Archangel Ariel Prayer Oil

2 drops ginger essential oil
6 drops orange essential oil
10 drops honeysuckle essential oil
1/8 cup extra virgin olive oil

A general prayer oil corresponding to all of Archangel Ariel's attributes - material needs, abundance, prosperity, healing and protecting the environment and wildlife.

Archangel Azrael Prayer Oil

8 drops rose or rose geranium essential oil
10 drops vanilla essential oil
1/8 cup extra virgin olive oil

A general prayer oil corresponding to all of Archangel Azrael's attributes - emotional healing, and to promote healing and support for grief over the loss of a loved one or pet.

Archangel Chamuel Prayer Oil

6 drops patchouli essential oil
12 drops Neroli essential oil
1/8 cup extra virgin olive oil

A general prayer oil corresponding to all of Archangel Chamuel's attributes - to find any lost item, to finding new love, a new job, new friends, a new home, and relationship healing.

Archangel Gabriel Prayer Oil

2 drops sweet orange essential oil
6 drops sandalwood essential oil
10 drops Jasmine essential oil
1/8 cup extra virgin olive oil

A general prayer oil corresponding to all of Archangel Gabriel's attributes - wisdom, confident decision-making, creative illumination, intelligence, and communication.

Archangel Haniel Prayer Oil

3 drops gardenia essential oil
3 drops sweet orange essential oil
6 drops sandalwood essential oil
6 drops tonka bean essential oil
1/8 cup extra virgin olive oil

A general prayer oil corresponding to all of Archangel Haniel's attributes - psychic awareness, peace, joy, harmony, creative inspiration, increasing productivity, meditation, and spirituality.

Archangel Jeremiel Prayer Oil

4 drops Jasmine essential oil
4 drops rose or rose geranium essential oil
10 drops sandalwood essential oil
1/8 cup extra virgin olive oil

A general prayer oil corresponding to all of Archangel Jeremiel's attributes - life purpose, problem-solving, clairvoyant dreams and visions, divine wisdom, spiritual wisdom, and spiritual awakening.

Archangel Jophiel Prayer Oil

4 drops sweet orange essential oil

4 drops ylang-ylang essential oil
10 drops patchouli essential oil
1/8 cup extra virgin olive oil

A general prayer oil corresponding to all of Archangel Jophiel's attributes - love, happiness, beauty, fertility, abundance, creativity, positive thinking and feeling, clearing subconscious clutter.

Archangel Metatron Prayer Oil

4 drops bergamot essential oil
4 drops lavender essential oil
10 drops rose or rose geranium essential oil
1/8 cup extra virgin olive oil

A general prayer oil corresponding to all of Archangel Metatron's attributes - spiritual growth, spiritual awareness, and spiritual and personal power.

Archangel Michael Prayer Oil

8 drops frankincense essential oil
8 drops sandalwood essential oil
2 drops sweet orange essential oil
1/8 cup extra virgin olive oil

A general prayer oil corresponding to all of Archangel Michael's attributes - courage, confidence, protection of any kind, purification, releasing of negative energy, and discovering life purpose.

Archangel Raguel Prayer Oil

4 drops clove essential oil
6 drops rosemary essential oil
8 drops Clary Sage essential oil
1/8 cup extra virgin olive oil

A general prayer oil corresponding to all of Archangel Raguel's attributes - justice, fairness, resolution to legal matters, restoring harmony relationships, resolving conflicts, and healing of arguments and misunderstandings.

Archangel Raphael Prayer Oil

7 drops rose or rose geranium essential oil
7 drops lavender essential oil
4 drops frankincense essential oil
1/8 cup extra virgin olive oil

A general prayer oil corresponding to all of Archangel Raphael's attributes - physical, emotional, mental, and spiritual healing, health, purification, healing of relationships, and healing of animals and pets.

Archangel Raziel Prayer Oil

6 drops cedarwood essential oil
6 drops frankincense essential oil
6 drops sandalwood essential oil
1/8 cup extra virgin off of oil

A general prayer oil corresponding to all of Archangel
Raziel's attributes - manifestation of desires, abundance,
prosperity, working with Universal Law, lucid dreaming,
dream interpretation, and spiritual wisdom.

Archangel Sandalphon Prayer Oil

2 drops Cedarwood essential oil
6 drops myrrh
10 drops frankincense
1/8 cup extra virgin olive oil

A general prayer oil corresponding to all of Archangel
Sandalphon attributes – supercharged prayer, peace and
serenity in difficult times, dispelling fear, and grounding.

Archangel Uriel Prayer Oil

2 drops lavender essential oil
6 drops thyme essential oil
10 drops peppermint essential oil

1/8 cup extra virgin olive oil

A general prayer oil corresponding to all of Archangel Uriel's attributes - spiritual wisdom, insight, and illumination, mental clarification, problem-solving, and creative ideas.

Archangel Zadkiel Prayer Oil

6 drops bergamot essential oil
6 drops rose or rose geranium essential oil
6 drops ylang-ylang
1/8 cup extra virgin olive oil

A general prayer oil corresponding to all of Archangel Zadkiel's attributes - unconditional forgiveness, compassion, healing of painful memories, and relationship healing.

Lotions and Ointments

I love the simplicity of making lotions and ointments. For that reason, I have included what I call "instant" lotion and ointment recipes in this book.

For these instant recipes, I use unscented body or face lotions and creams which are easily purchased from your local grocery or drug store.

For the instant ointments, I switch between two products called Waxelen and the other TD Naturals Healthy Jelly.

Both are all-natural, nonpetroleum-based ointments. They have the consistency of petroleum jelly but absorbs into the skin smoother without the slight greasy residual. Both products can be purchased online.

Of course, alternatively, you can use petroleum jelly if you desire with the following ointment recipes.

How to Make Your Own Lotion or Ointment Base

Ointment Recipe - Yields 2 oz.

The best ointment recipes contained beeswax (alternatively you may use Carnauba Wax flakes for a vegan option, or if you are allergic to bee products) and a good organic vegetable oil such as extra virgin olive oil, almond oil, or safflower oil. Ointments are generally stored in smaller containers in jars. Because of this, I have included a recipe that yields a small amount of about ¼ cup of the final product.

Ingredients:

4 Tablespoons of Beeswax (or Carnauba Wax flakes)
Organic vegetable oil of your choice
A small microwave-safe glass bowl or measuring cup

Place the wax chips or shavings in the glass bowl or measuring cup, and slowly pour the oil in the container just to the point that it covers the wax. Do not overfill with oil!

Heat in the microwave for about a minute to one minute and thirty seconds. Stir every 20 to 30 seconds with a wooden utensil such as a chopstick, Popsicle stick, or wooden skewer. Watch carefully. As soon the wax melts you are done. Do not overheat.

Add the essential oils of your choice (or those found in the following recipes) stir gently, and cover. Place in the refrigerator to cool. The resulting solid will have the consistency of petroleum jelly.

Optional: add one drop of tincture of Benzoin. Benzoin acts as a natural preservative.

Once cooled transfer ointment into a small glass or plastic jar or container. Store your ointments in a cool, dark place. Discard if any mold appears.

Basic Lotion Recipe – Yields 4 oz.

2 Tablespoons Coconut Oil
2 Tablespoons Shea Butter
1 Tablespoon of Essential Oils of your choice (or those that are found in the following recipes)

Blend all ingredients together in a bullet style personal blender. Optional: add two drops of tincture of benzoin as a preservative.

Spoon into a 4-ounce glass jar or plastic container. Store in refrigerator for up to six months. Discard if any mold appears.

Lotion Recipes

The following recipes yield approximately 4 ounces of lotion. Store in an airtight jar or container.

Caution: do not use citrus essential oils in a homemade body lotion prior to prolonged exposure in the sun. Citrus oils can increase the risk of sunburn.

Archangel Sandalphon Lavender and Sage Body Lotion

6 drops Clary Sage essential oil
10 drops lavender essential oil
unscented lotion

Mix all ingredients until well blended. The calming effects of lavender and the relaxing benefits of sage will help you unwind and restore mental and emotional balance. Use to quiet your mind and soothe your senses!

Archangel Chamuel Romantic Love Body Lotion

6 drops essential oil patchouli
10 drops essential oil of vanilla
unscented lotion

Mix all ingredients until well blended. Use to enhance the love vibration in romantic relationships. This body lotion is also very soothing and relaxing to the body-mind.

Archangel Jophiel Mood Lifting Body Lotion

4 drops rose essential oil
4 drops orange essential oil
8 drops sandalwood essential oil
unscented lotion

Mix all ingredients until well blended. Use to lift your mood and brighten your day. This body lotion is also very soothing during times of anxiety or depression.

Archangel Raphael Lavender after Sun Relief

15 drops lavender essential oil
4-ounces plain yogurt
1-ounce aloe vera gel

Mix all ingredients in a small glass or ceramic bowl until combined. For soothing relief after a day in the sun apply directly to skin and allow to dry; rinse off with cool water. Repeat as often as desired. Store in refrigerator after use. Do not eat.

Archangel Azrael Vanilla Delight Lotion

4 drops benzoin essential oil
12 drops vanilla essential oil
unscented lotion

Mix all ingredients until well blended. Use to luxuriate in Archangel Azrael's loving presence, as well as to help you move through the grieving process.

Archangel Jophiel Vanilla Rose Romantic Body Lotion

6 drops vanilla essential oil
10 drops rose or rose geranium essential oil
unscented lotion

Mix all ingredients until well blended. This is a very sensual, and sexy body lotion!

Archangel Jophiel Sweet Orange Hand Lotion

2 drops Roman chamomile essential oil
14 drops sweet orange essential oil
unscented lotion

Mix all ingredients until well blended. Use to soothe dry, chapped hands. The fragrance is also very soothing and calming to the mind and body.

Archangel Sandalphon Calming Body Lotion

1 drop vanilla essential oil
5 drops lavender essential oil

10 drops sweet orange essential oil
unscented lotion

Mix all ingredients until well blended. Use to calm racing
thoughts, as well as to relax the body.

Archangel Raphael Moisturizing Cream

1 drop lavender essential oil
4 drops sandalwood essential oil
4 drops sweet orange essential oil
6 drops rose essential oil
½ teaspoon vitamin E oil
unscented lotion

Mix all ingredients until well blended. This fragrant blend
leaves the skin soft, smooth, and silky.

Archangel Raphael Soothing Foot Lotion

6 drops lavender essential oil
10 drops peppermint essential oil
unscented lotion

Mix all ingredients until well blended. Use to soften dry,
cracked feet.

Archangel Jophiel Sensuous Lotion

2 drops rose essential oil
4 drops lemon essential oil
4 drops sweet orange essential oil
6 drops sandalwood essential oil
unscented lotion

Mix all ingredients until well blended. A fabulously fragrant body lotion sure to set the tone for romantic evening with that special someone.

Archangel Chamuel New Beginnings Lotion

4 drops cardamom essential oil
4 drops sweet orange essential oil
6 drops sandalwood essential oil
6 drops vanilla essential oil
unscented lotion

Mix all ingredients until well blended. Use whenever you are beginning something new – new relationships, new job, new friends . . . etc. Also a perfect lotion for the special man in your life.

Archangel Raziel Sweet Dreams Lotion

4 drops Clary Sage essential oil
4 drops rose geranium essential oil
8 drops bergamot essential oil
unscented lotion

Mix all ingredients until well blended. For a peaceful night's rest use prior to sleep.

Archangel Michael Protect Me Body Lotion

2 drops vanilla essential oil
4 drops sandalwood essential oil
6 drops frankincense essential oil
6 drops myrrh essential oil
unscented lotion

Mix all ingredients until well blended. Use to protect and shield your bio energetic body from negative influences.

Archangel Sandalphon Ground Me Body Lotion

4 drops sweet orange essential oil
6 drops lavender essential oil
6 drops rosemary essential oil
unscented lotion

Mix all ingredients until well blended. Use to ground your physical and emotional energy.

Archangel Raziel Abundance Body Lotion

2 drops jasmine essential oil
2 drops patchouli essential oil
4 drops sandalwood essential oil
6 drops vanilla essential oil
unscented lotion

Mix all ingredients until well blended. This rich body lotion smells like a million bucks!

Archangel Zadkiel Soul Soothing Body Lotion

6 drops lavender essential oil
10 drops Roman chamomile essential oil
unscented lotion

Mix all ingredients until well blended. A very soul calming, emotionally healing, and soothing body lotion.

Ointment Recipes

The following recipes yield approximately 2 ounces of ointment. Store in an airtight jar or container.

Caution: do not use citrus essential oils in a homemade ointment prior to prolonged exposure in the sun. Citrus oils can increase the risk of sunburn.

Archangel Raphael "Boo-Boo" Ointment

5 drops calendula essential oil
5 drops lavender essential oil
6 drops tea tree oil
unscented ointment

Mix all ingredients well until blended. This blend is heaven's answer to Neosporin®.

Archangel Jophiel Love Your Skin Ointment

8 drops Roman chamomile essential oil
8 drops rose essential oil
unscented ointment

Mix all ingredients well until blended. Use to soothe and soften excessively dry or chapped skin.

Archangel Raphael Headache Relieving Ointment

8 drops lavender essential oil
8 drops peppermint essential oil
unscented ointment

Mix all ingredients until well blended. To alleviate headache caused by tension apply a small amount to your temples, and neck.

Archangel Zadkiel Sleep Soundly Ointment

2 drops sweet orange essential oil
8 drops lavender essential oil
8 drops Roman chamomile essential oil
unscented ointment

Mix all ingredients until well blended. Apply a small amount to your neck and shoulders prior to sleep. For occasional insomnia apply a small amount to your neck and shoulders.

Archangel Zadkiel Lucid Dreams Ointment

2 drops lemon essential oil
8 drops chamomile essential oil
8 drops Mugwort essential oil
unscented ointment

Mix all ingredients until well blended. Helps to promote Lucid dreams. This ointment is also wonderful for relieving menstrual cramps. Caution - do not use during pregnancy.

Archangel Ariel Bugs Be Gone Ointment

6 drops lemon essential oil
10 drops rose geranium essential oil
unscented ointment

Mix all ingredients until well blended. A pleasant, fragrant all-natural insect repellent. To use, apply a thin amount to skin exposed to the elements. Massage into skin until absorbed.

Archangel Raphael Healing Balm Ointment

2 drops cinnamon essential oil
4 drops white camphor essential oil
4 drops peppermint essential oil
6 drops eucalyptus
unscented ointment

Mix all ingredients until well blended. Heaven's answer to Tiger Balm®. Rub into sore muscles and joints. Also great for chest congestion due to the common cold. When applying this ointment start with about a pea sized dab; a little of this ointment goes a long way!

Archangel Sandalphon Calming Ointment

2 drops Roman chamomile essential oil
4 drops lemon essential oil
10 drops lavender essential oil
unscented ointment

Mix all ingredients until well blended. To regain a sense of peace and serenity, especially after a hectic day, rub a small amount into your temples, and behind your ears.

Teas and Potions

There's something magical about a hot steaming cup of tea on a cold evening. I enjoy the feel of my mug as it rests on the table between my palms. The steam rising from my mug dances in the cool air bringing with it a beautiful bouquet of tranquility. I am in bliss!

The following recipes are a collection of heavenly teas meant for the Zen of sensuous sipping, as well as a few 'potions' which consist of a few simple simmering potpourri recipes intended to lift and clear the energies in your living space.

The simmering potpourris are not meant for drinking but have been included in this section because they are basically an herbal infusion such as the tea recipes shared in the following pages of this book.

Common Tea Bases

As with the other recipes I have shared up to this point, I am a fan of 'instant recipes' or those that can be prepared in a short amount of time. For that reason, I have used a prepared tea base for the recipes in this chapter. These prepared tea bases are the type you can find at your local grocery.

Of course, I have also included simple standalone herbal tea recipes that are also easy to make and stimulating to the senses.

As far as varieties of teas there are six main groups: white, green, oolong, black, pu'erh, and yerba maté. What accounts for the variety and difference in tea groups is the length of time leaves are oxidized and the processing style which can include methods such as roasting, steaming, and pan firing.

White Tea – White teas are very subtle in flavor, very delicate and very light. They are the least processed of all teas. When brewed and combined with other herbs the result is a very light smooth tea.

Green Tea - Traditionally green teas are from China and Japan. The lack of oxidation accounts for the teas green color as well as low caffeine count. There are many varieties of green teas, some flavored and some scented. Green tea is one of my favorite tea bases as it pairs well with most dried herbs especially those that are sweet and spicy.

Oolong Teas – Oolong teas are semi-oxidized, which places it in a category midway between green and black teas. From lightly oxidized to lightly roasted, oolong can be frequently floral to lusciously rich. Like green tea, oolongs combined wonderfully with sweet and spicy herbs.

Black Tea – Basic black teas, as well as flavored black teas, make some great bases for instant "herbal" tea brews. Along with herbs and spices, black teas can be flavored by adding fresh or dried fruit peels, fruit juices, or floral essences. They pair well with all herbs and spices.

Pu'erh Teas – Pu'erh teas are very smooth in taste. They are aged and fermented and are available in both green and black varieties. Throughout Asia, these teas are revered for their medicinal benefits. The flavor of this tea can be light with the green variety to intensely earthy with the black variety. Pairs well with bolder spices and herbs.

Yerba Maté – Yerba Maté is similar to green tea in taste and is very healthy and stimulating to drink. As an added benefit it serves as an appetite suppressant. Like green teas, maté pairs well with most dried herbs, especially those that are sweet and spicy

Basic Tea Base

Mix the ingredients in a glass jar or similar airtight container. To use, measure 1 to 2 teaspoons per cup of boiling water. Feel free to add more if you prefer stronger brews. Put loose tea in a tea strainer and let steep for a minimum of 3 to 5 minutes, or longer if you prefer stronger tea.

Tea strainers come in a variety of styles such as tea ball strainers, spoon strainers, as well as mug type strainers which fit perfectly inside your mug or teacup.

Tip: use pure spring water whenever possible! Pure, fresh water makes all the difference when it comes to a good cup of tea.

For a 2 cup tea pot use up to 1 tablespoon and let steep for 5 to 10 minutes per your preference of strength and taste.

Optionally sweeten your tea with honey, sugar, Stevia, or other desired sweetener, and/or add milk or creamer.

Tea Recipes

Archangel Haniel Clairvoyant Tea

2 teaspoons chamomile
1 teaspoon cinnamon
1 teaspoon mugwort
honey to taste

Add dried herbs into one cup of boiling water. Steep for 2 to 3 minutes while asking Archangel Haniel to open your intuitive senses. Sweetened with honey to taste. Use whenever you want to strengthen your psychic senses.

Archangel Uriel Inner Illumination Tea ✳

¼ cup fresh ginger, thinly sliced
2 cinnamon sticks
2 tablespoons honey
6 cups of water
optional lemon wedges (to garnish)

Simmer ginger, honey, cinnamon, and water for 20 minutes. Strain tea before serving. Drink whenever you need an added boost of inner clarity in regards to particular situation or circumstance.

Archangel Michael Soothing Christmas Tea

1 cinnamon stick
1/2 teaspoon whole cloves
1 tablespoon lemon juice
3 black tea bags
¼ cup sugar
½ cup orange juice
3 cups of water

Add all ingredients except tea bags into a pot and bring to a boil. Take pot off heat, add teabags, and let steep to preference. Remove cloves, cinnamon, and teabags and serve. Makes 2 to 4 servings.

Archangel Haniel Heart Opening Tea

1 teaspoon ginger powder
2 teaspoons dried rosemary
2 cups boiling water
honey to taste

Mix all ingredients well and steep in 2 cups boiling water for eight minutes. Sweetened to taste with honey. Drink to loosen tension in your heart, and to awaken feelings of love and tenderness. Makes 2 servings.

Archangel Jophiel Relaxing Vanilla Rose Tea

1 teaspoon pure vanilla extract
2 tablespoons dried rose petals (gourmet)
2 ½ cups boiling water
honey to taste

Pour all ingredients into a large mug or teapot. Stir well and let steep for 30 minutes. Strain, and serve. You may reheat the strained tea if necessary. Drink a cup of this delicious aromatic and relaxing tea whenever you need to unwind and soothe the senses.

Simmering Potpourri Recipes

Simmering Potpourri recipes are a fantastic way to make your living space smell warm and inviting, especially around the holiday season when fragrant spices such as cinnamon, cloves, and allspice are most often used.

Basic Directions for Making Simmering Potpourri

Making simmering potpourris is also simple. Fill up a large saucepan with 6 cups of water and bring to a boil. Add the ingredients from your chosen recipe, and continue to boil for approximately three minutes. Next, turn the heat to the lowest setting possible to simmer. For best results simmer for about 1 to 1.5 hours. It is more than enough time to brighten your living space with pleasant, aromatic fragrances.

Caution: DO NOT DRINK! Whenever possible keep the saucepan on the farthest burner to avoid contact with children or pets. Keep an eye on the level of liquid in the pan to avoid the pot burning dry. Also, never leave your home with the mixture still simmering on the stove.

Archangel Haniel Harmony Simmering Potpourri

1 tablespoon whole cloves
2 cinnamon sticks
1 small apple quartered
1 small orange quartered
4 drops cinnamon essential oil
2 drops sweet orange essential oil
1 drop clove essential oil

Use to promote harmony and love in your living space. A perfect simmering potpourri to use when entertaining.

Archangel Jophiel Happy Vibes Simmering Potpourri

2 cinnamon sticks
1 medium orange quartered
1 tablespoon pure vanilla extract
4 drops vanilla essential oil
2 drops sweet orange essential oil

Use to fill your living space with happy, loving, joyful vibrations.

Archangel Gabriel Clarity Simmering Potpourri

4 six inch sprigs of fresh rosemary
1 medium lemon quartered

6 drops lemon essential oil

Use to create an environment that is mentally and emotionally clear and invigorating. A wonderful simmering potpourri to use during any creative endeavor.

Archangel Raphael Room Purifying Simmering Potpourri

1 tablespoons whole cloves
2 cinnamon sticks
6 star anise
1 medium orange quartered
3 drops clove essential oil
2 drops orange essential oil
1 drop cinnamon essential oil

Although this simmering potpourri smells just like the winter holidays, it also doubles as an antifungal and antibacterial secret agent.

Archangel Metatron Personal Power Simmering Potpourri

4 six inch sprigs of fresh rosemary
4 six inch sprigs of fresh lavender
2 bay leaves
1 medium lemon quartered
3 drops lavender essential oil
2 drops lemon essential oil

Do you need to clear your mind and catch up on you? This simmering potpourri is the perfect answer. The aroma is fresh, clean, and decisive.

Archangel Chamuel Hopeful Simmering Potpourri

4 six inch sprigs fresh lavender
2 cups dried rose petals
1 tablespoon whole cloves
1 tablespoon ground nutmeg
1 cinnamon stick broken into pieces
4 drops rose geranium essential oil
4 drops patchouli essential oil
4 drops Jasmine essential oil

Use to remain hopeful and inspired when waiting for new opportunities including new love, a new job, or a new home. This simmering potpourri is also wonderful to use while meditating, or while practicing a moving meditation such as yoga, tai chi, or chi gong.

Archangel Michael Protect This Space Simmering Potpourri

2 tablespoons whole cloves
2 tablespoons allspice
2 cinnamon sticks
2 drops clove essential oil
1 drop cinnamon essential oil

Use to protect your living space from negative energies and unwelcome entities.

Archangel Ariel Prosperity Simmering Potpourri

½ cups dried jasmine blossoms
1 medium orange quartered
1 cinnamon stick broken into pieces
4 drops Jasmine essential oil
2 drops orange essential oil

Use to remind yourself about how prosperous and abundant you already are in all areas of your life. This fragrance is sexy – sweet yet slightly spicy; a perfect combination for a romantic evening!

Notes:

Bath Soaps, Soaks, and Salts

I don't know about you, for me, it's the little things in life that bring the most pleasure. Giving myself permission to soak in a hot tub of water is one of these things.

There are many therapeutic benefits of soaking the body in a tub of hot water; some of which may surprise you.

The Benefits of Hot Baths

Improving your blood circulation. Soaking your body in hot water is good for your heart. When you are inside the water your heart works faster and stronger, increasing the blood flow throughout your body.

Relaxes the body and mind. Nothing is more relaxing than a hot bath at the end of a long day. It is a great stress reliever, causing tense muscles to relax, and mental and emotional tension to melt away. It is also a great sleeping aid.

Healing and soothing overworked muscles and joints. Physical activity is a necessity for living. And sometimes injuries due to muscle overuse, and joint pain resulting from everyday wear and tear on the body can keep you from performing at your best.

A hot bath is a perfect ending to arduous physical activity and is very healing and soothing to the body as well.

Lowers your blood pressure. Recent medical studies have shown that soaking in a hot bath can lower your blood pressure. The hot water effect on relaxing your muscles and melting away your stress evens out spikes in your blood pressure; helping you to return to a state of peaceful bliss. Obviously, however, if you have a heart condition you should check with your physician prior to beginning a bath regimen.

Purifying and cleansing your skin. A decent soak in hot water after showering will open up the pores of your skin. Also, a good soak in hot water releases the dirt and toxins in your skin. This results in cleaner and more youthful looking skin.

The therapeutic effects of a hot bath are intensified when using herbal and aromatherapy bath soaks, soaps, and salts. It is a heavenly way to recharge and reset your emotional vibrations as well as to ground yourself physically.

Also one can agree that taking baths (and showers too) are fun; especially when you share your tub or shower with that special someone. Wink! Wink!

Basic Soap Base

The soap recipes shared in this book use melt and pour soap. This is basically an instant soap base that you melt, adding your herbs and or essential oils to the mixture just prior to pouring into a mold.

The beauty of melt and pour soap bases is that you can make your own soap in a few hours. You can find melt and pour soap bases online in many varieties, and may also purchase them from many craft stores such as Michael's and Hobby Lobby.

The soap recipes included in this book can be used with the soap base of your choice.

Ingredients:

• 1 pound of soap base of your choice
• 4 cup microwave-safe measuring cup or glass bowl
• cutting board
• rubbing alcohol in a small spray bottle
• serrated knife
• small wire whisk
• plastic wrap
• microwave
• soap molds

1. Cut the soap into 1-inch cubes for easier melting. For a cutting guide, most soap bases have 1-inch gridlines already embedded on the top of the soap base. 1 pound of melt and pour soap base will make four 4 ounce bars of soap, or numerous smaller soaps depending on the type of mold you use.

2. Put the chunks of soap base into your microwave-safe measuring cup or bowl. Cover with plastic wrap, and heat in the microwave on high for 30 to 45 seconds. If the base isn't quite melted, stir it with your whisk gently and then continue to heat at 10-second intervals, gently stirring in between until the mixture is fully melted. Important! You need to replace the plastic wrap each time you place the glass container back into the microwave.

3. Remove the soap base from the microwave. Gently stir in the recipe ingredients. Don't stir too hard or fast as you will create excess air bubbles.

4. Slowly pour your soap base into the mold. There are a wide variety of soap molds available in the marketplace but you can use heat resistant muffin trays, tart hands, and even plastic travel soap containers.

5. Lightly spray the top of your soap mixture with rubbing alcohol to eliminate excess bubbles. Do not over spray.

6. Let the mixture sit for several hours at room temperature to solidify, or place in refrigerator for about two hours. When the soap mixture has fully hardened remove them from the molds and enjoy!

Bath Salt Base

Ingredients:

*   2 cups Epsom Salts
*   ½ cup baking soda
*   ¼ sea salt (optional)

Mix all ingredients in a glass bowl. Add the essential oils and/or herbs and mix well. Store in an airtight glass jar or container. Use ¼ cup per bath.

Bath Soap Recipes

Archangel Michael Purifying Soap

1 teaspoon vitamin E oil
1 ½ teaspoon ground cinnamon
1 drop Rosemary essential oil
5 drops orange essential oil
10 drops lavender essential oil
1 pound melt and pour soap of your choice

This soap recipe is fabulous for its antibacterial and antifungal properties. Use as a general all-purpose purifying soap.

Archangel Jophiel Oatmeal and Honey Soap

2 teaspoons honey
3 teaspoons vanilla essential oil
¼ cup ground, rolled oats
1 pound melt and pour soap of your choice

A wonderful and relaxing soap base that not only softens and nourishes your skin, but also exfoliates.

Archangel Metatron Green Tea Lavender Soap

3 teaspoons lavender essential oil
1 tablespoons dried lavender
1 tablespoon green tea (or contents of one green tea bag)
1 pound melt and pour soap of your choice

A pleasing, fragrant soap base that is sure to perk up your personal power! One of my absolute favorites!

Archangel Gabriel Bergamot Tea Soap

1 ½ teaspoons bergamot essential oil

1 ½ teaspoons lemon essential oil
1 tablespoon bergamot mint (or contents of one Earl Grey teabag)
1 pound melt and pour soap of your choice

As an author and creative this soap base always has a way of churning my creative juices. This soap is not only very relaxing, but stimulating to the senses as well.

Archangel Haniel Rosemary Lemon Soap

1 teaspoon Rosemary essential oil
1 teaspoon lemon essential oil
1 tablespoon ground Rosemary
1 pound melt and pour soap of your choice

As a professional psychic and psychic medium I often perform pre-client meditations the night before our scheduled appointment. Many times I perform my pre-client meditation while relaxing in the bath. This soap base helps to open your third eye and heightens your psychic senses.

Archangel Azrael Sweetest Dreams Soap

1 teaspoon Roman chamomile essential oil
1 teaspoon sweet orange essential oil
1 tablespoon chamomile (or contents of one chamomile herbal tea bag)

1 pound melt and pour soap of your choice

Having trouble sleeping? Using this soap just prior to falling asleep will relax you and help to promote a peaceful night's sleep.

Archangel Ariel Wake Me up Soap

1 teaspoon peppermint essential oil
2 teaspoons Rosemary essential oil
1 tablespoon of dried peppermint (or contents of one peppermint herbal tea bag)
1 pound melt and pour soap of your choice

An invigorating, eye-opening soap base that is sure to wake you up, and point your day in the right direction.

Archangel Raphael Lavender Oatmeal Soap

3 teaspoons lavender essential oil
1 tablespoon dried lavender
¼ cup ground, rolled oats
1 pound melt and pour soap of your choice

This soap base is soothing to the skin, and healing to the spirit. Perfect for use after a long hectic workday.

Bath Salt Recipes

Archangel Raphael Stress Relieving Bath Salt

1/3 cup Himalayan pink salt
1/3 cup Epsom salts
¼ cup baking soda
10 drops chamomile essential oil
8 drops sweet orange essential oil
6 drops sandalwood essential oil

Mix all ingredients well. Sprinkle one ¼ to ½ cups into hot bath water. Store excess in an airtight container or jar. Use to soak away mental and emotional stress and strain.

Archangel Michael Deep Psychic Cleansing Bath Salt

1 drop clove essential oil
2 tablespoons Rosemary
3 tablespoons sandalwood
3 tablespoons frankincense
Basic Bath Salt Recipe

Mix all ingredients well. Sprinkle one ¼ to ½ cups into hot bath water. Store excess in an airtight container or jar. Use for a deep cleansing of your bioenergetic body. Note - do not use more than one drop of the clove essential oil as it will irritate your skin!

Archangel Raphael Healing Bath Salt

1 tablespoon sandalwood
2 tablespoons eucalyptus
3 tablespoons dried orange peel
Basic Bath Salt Recipe

Mix all ingredients well. Sprinkle one ¼ to ½ cups into hot bath water. Store excess in an airtight container or jar. Use to help facilitate a speedy recovery from illness.

Archangel Metatron Higher Consciousness Bath Salt

1 tablespoon frankincense
2 tablespoons sandalwood
3 tablespoons Cedar wood
Basic Bath Salt Recipe

Mix all ingredients well. Sprinkle one ¼ to ½ cups into hot bath water. Store excess in an airtight container or jar. Use to tune into higher spiritual awareness.

Archangel Jophiel Lovers Bath Salt

2 drops sandalwood essential oil
6 drops geranium essential oil
10 drops Palmarosa essential oil
2 tablespoons dried lavender
Basic Bath Salt Recipe

Mix all ingredients well. Sprinkle one ¼ to ½ cups into hot bath water. Store excess in an airtight container or jar. Use to attract love and to expand your ability to give and to receive love.

Archangel Haniel Deep Meditation Bath Salt

1 tablespoon frankincense
2 tablespoons Rosemary
3 tablespoons geranium
Basic Bath Salt Recipe

Mix all ingredients well. Sprinkle one ¼ to ½ cups into hot bath water. Store excess in an airtight container or jar. Use to relax the mind prior to meditation practice.

Archangel Ariel Abundant Bliss Bath Salt

20 drops lavender essential oil
10 drops peppermint essential oil
3 tablespoons dried lavender
Basic Bath Salt Recipe

Mix all ingredients well. Sprinkle one ¼ to ½ cups into hot bath water. Store excess in an airtight container or jar. This is a very stimulating bath salt blend. Use to increase your prosperity and abundance vibes!

Archangel Raphael All Purpose Healing Bath Salt

15 drops geranium essential oil
20 drops sandalwood essential oil
1 cup dried rose petals
Basic Bath Salt Recipe

Mix all ingredients well. Sprinkle one ¼ to ½ cups into hot bath water. Store excess in an airtight container or jar. A general all-purpose bath salt that is aromatic, and healing to the mind, body, and soul.

Archangel Jophiel Relaxed and Renewed Bath Salt

10 drops geranium essential oil
10 drops Jasmine essential oil
10 drops ylang-ylang essential oil
Basic Bath Salt Recipe

Mix all ingredients well. Sprinkle one ¼ to ½ cups into hot bath water. Store excess in an airtight container or jar. Use to relax and unwind after a stressful day. This bath salt blend is also perfect to share with your lover or significant other.

Bath "Soaks" Recipes

Bath "soaks" are herbal and salt bath blends using a combination of dried herbs, essential oils and bath salts. I have included several bath recipes in the Oils chapter of this book, but wanted to make sure that I added the following recipes – simply because they are my favorites!

Archangel Raphael Purification Herbal Bath Soak

2 tablespoons basil
2 tablespoons rosemary
1 tablespoon yarrow
1 tablespoon cumin
cotton muslin bag or piece of cheese cloth, or nylon stocking

To cleanse yourself from negative energy, mix all ingredients together in a small bowl, then either fill a muslin cotton bag with the mixture, or wrap herbs in a piece of cheese cloth or nylon stocking. Secure with a piece of string. Place herbs in your bath water and let sit for 10 minutes before entering.

Archangel Raphael Aura Cleansing Bath

8 drops orange essential oil
12 drops sandalwood essential oil
½ cup sea salt
½ cup baking soda

To cleanse your aura, or bioenergetic body, add all ingredients into a tub of hot bath water. Light a white candle (optional), and ask for Archangel Raphael's assistance while holding the intention of cleansing and clearing your auric layers. Soak for 20 minutes and then rinse your body thoroughly with clear water.

Archangel Raphael Spring Cleansing Bath

12 drops sage essential oil
12 drops rose geranium essential oil
½ cup Epsom salts
½ cup baking soda

Add all ingredients in a hot water bath, and soak for 20 minutes. Rinse your body thoroughly afterwards with clear hot water. Used to welcome the fresh energy of spring and all of its abundant blessings!

Archangel Chamuel Inner Peace Bath Oil Blend

6 drops grapefruit essential oil
6 drops bergamot essential oil
6 drops lime essential oil
4 drops ginger essential oil
2 drops essential oil of sandalwood

Blend all oils together. Store in an airtight glass vial or container. Place the drops of oil directly into your bathwater whenever you feel a need to decompress after a stressful day.

Archangel Sandalphon Root Chakra Bath Oil

10 drops Oak Moss essential oil
20 drops vetiver essential oil
30 drops myrrh essential oil

Place the drops of oil directly into a hot bath. Ask Archangel Chamuel to ground, cleanse, and balance your root chakra. A balanced root chakra provides you with a stable foundation on which you fortify yourself physically, mentally and emotionally. The root chakra is responsible for grounding your energies to the earth as well as anchoring your personal energy into the world.

Archangel Chamuel Sacral Chakra Balancing Bath Oil

16 drops roast geranium essential oil
12 drops sweet orange essential oil
10 drops sandalwood essential oil
10 drops ylang-ylang essential oil

Place the drops of oil directly into a hot bath. Ask Archangel Chamuel to ground and tonify your second chakra. Your sacral chakra is related to your emotions, your relationships with others, in your sexuality. A healthy second chakra brings balanced emotions, creative fulfillment, and satisfying relationships.

Archangel Uriel Solar Plexus Chakra Balancing Bath Oil

16 drops geranium essential oil
20 drops bergamot essential oil
20 drops sweet orange essential oil

Place the drops of oil directly into a hot bath. Ask Archangel Uriel to cleanse and balance your Solar Plexus Chakra. A healthy solar plexus chakra allows you to move through life with courage and confidence. Also, use to stimulate spiritual joy, wisdom, and insight. This bath oil blend is intoxicating!

Archangel Raphael Heart Chakra Balancing Bath Oil

10 drops Jasmine essential oil
30 drops sandalwood essential oil
30 drops ylang-ylang essential oil

Place the drops of oil directly into a hot bath. Ask Archangel Raphael to cleanse and balance your heart chakra. A healthy heart chakra allows you to give and receive love in a balanced, healthy way. A balanced heart chakra also enables you to expand and grow in spiritual love.

Archangel Michael Throat Chakra Balancing Bath Oil

10 drops Roman chamomile essential oil
10 drops basil essential oil
30 drops bergamot essential oil

Place the drops of oil directly into a hot bath. Ask Archangel Michael to cleanse and balance your throat chakra. A healthy throat chakra allows for honest, open communication to other people as well with that of God and the angels.

Archangel Gabriel Third Eye Balancing Bath Oil

10 drops sandalwood essential oil
20 drops Juniper essential oil
30 drops Rosemary essential oil

Place the drops of oil directly into a hot bath. Ask Archangel Gabriel to cleanse and balance your third eye chakra. Your third eye or sixth chakra, is the seat of your intuition. A healthy third eye chakra can enable clairvoyance, telepathy, expanded consciousness, lucid dreaming, and visualization.

Archangel Zadkiel Crown Chakra Balancing Bath Oil

10 drops sandalwood essential oil
30 drops frankincense essential oil
30 drops myrrh essential oil

Place the drops of oil directly into a hot bath. Ask Archangel Zadkiel to cleanse and balance your crown chakra. The crown chakra is your energetic connection to the universe. The seventh chakra is responsible for dispersing universal life force energy into the other six chakras below it. A balanced seventh chakra allows you to intimately connect to God's love, as well as to easily receive Divine Guidance.

Archangel Sandalphon Sweet Life Herbal Bath Soak

3 drops geranium essential oil
3 drops lavender essential oil
3 drops lemongrass essential oil
2 tablespoons sassafras
2 tablespoons whole cloves
1/2 cup dried lavender
1/2 cup dried lemongrass

To revel in the sweetness of life with heartfelt gratitude mix all ingredients together in a small bowl, then either fill a muslin cotton bag with the mixture, or wrap herbs in a piece of cheese cloth or nylon stocking.

Secure with a piece of string. Place herbs in your bath water and let sit for 10 minutes before entering. For best results place herbal mixture in an airtight container and let sit for 24 hours prior to use.

Archangel Jophiel Happiness Herbal Bath Soak

3 drops lavender essential oil
4 drops rose geranium essential oil
1/4 cup loose green tea
1/2 cup dried lavender
1/2 cup dried rose petals

To promote thoughts of love and happiness mix all ingredients together in a small bowl, then either fill a muslin cotton bag with the mixture, or wrap herbs in a piece of cheese cloth or nylon stocking. Secure with a piece of string. Place herbs in your bath water and let sit for 10 minutes before entering. For best results place herbal mixture in an airtight container and let sit for 24 hours prior to use.

Archangel Raphael Healing Bliss Herbal Bath Soak

½ cup dried lavender
½ cup dried rose petals
½ cup oatmeal
4 drops Palmarosa essential oil
6 drops lavender essential oil

To rebalance yourself physically, emotionally, mentally, and spiritually, mix all ingredients together in a small bowl, then either fill a muslin cotton bag with the mixture, or wrap herbs in a piece of cheese cloth or nylon stocking. Secure with a piece of string. Place herbs in your bath water and let sit for 10 minutes before entering. For best results place herbal mixture in an airtight container and let sit for 24 hours prior to use.

Archangel Metatron Spiritual Splendor Herbal Bath Soak

1/4 cup bay leaves
1/4 cup dried lavender
1/4 cup dried mint
1/4 cup dried Rosemary
1/4 cup dried sage
1/4 cup dried thyme

To promote spiritual wisdom and understanding mix all ingredients together in a small bowl, then either fill a muslin cotton bag with the mixture, or wrap herbs in a piece of cheese cloth or nylon stocking. Secure with a piece of string. Place herbs in your bath water and let sit for 10 minutes before entering.

Archangel Jeremiel Divine Wisdom Herbal Bath Soak
4 drops rosemary essential oil

6 drops basil essential oil
½ cup dried basil
½ cup dried rosemary
1 cup oatmeal

For divine wisdom and enhanced spiritual vision mix all ingredients together in a small bowl, then either fill a muslin cotton bag with the mixture, or wrap herbs in a piece of cheese cloth or nylon stocking. Secure with a piece of string. Place herbs in your bath water and let sit for 10 minutes before entering. For best results place herbal mixture in an airtight container and let sit for 24 hours prior to use.

Archangel Chamuel Relax My Mind Herbal Bath Soak

½ cup dried chamomile
½ cup dried lavender
1 cup powdered milk

To help promote patience, and relax racing thoughts mix all ingredients together in a small bowl, then either fill a muslin cotton bag with the mixture, or wrap herbs in a piece of cheese cloth or nylon stocking. Secure with a piece of string. Place herb and milk mixture in your bath water and let sit for 10 minutes before entering.

Archangel Michael Negativity Releasing Herbal Bath Soak

¼ cup dried Rose petals
¼ cup dried lavender
¼ cup dried orange peel
½ cup powdered milk
1 cup oatmeal

To help release any negative energy you have picked up throughout the day mix all ingredients together in a small bowl, then either fill a muslin cotton bag with the mixture, or wrap herbs in a piece of cheese cloth or nylon stocking. Secure with a piece of string. Place herbal mixture in your bath water and let sit for 10 minutes before entering.

Archangel Gabriel Confusion Clearing Herbal Bath Soak

¼ cup dried calendula flowers
¼ cup eucalyptus
½ cup lemongrass
1 cup oatmeal

To clear away mental stress and confusion mix all ingredients together in a small bowl, then either fill a muslin cotton bag with the mixture, or wrap herbs in a piece of cheese cloth or nylon stocking. Secure with a piece of string. Place herbs in your bath water and let sit for 10 minutes before entering.

Herbal Sachets, Potpourri, and Angel Charms

Herbal sachets and potpourri mixes are fun to make and are also great to give away as gifts.

I place my empowered sachets, charms, or potpourri on my personal altar and enjoy their fragrant essences as I meditate and pray.

Sachets are small cloth bags filled with scented herbs or potpourri. You can make them in various sizes.

Many of the recipes in this chapter suggest the use of a sachet bag in a color that corresponds with a specific Archangel, but this is optional. Feel free to use any color of your choice. You can purchase multicolor sachet bags online and from many craft and party stores.

Angel charms are smaller herbal sachets that contain a small quartz crystal. The crystal and herbs are wrapped inside of a 2-inch square piece of fabric and tied with the string or ribbon. For fun, I sometimes add a small metallic charm corresponding with my intention on the string or ribbon wrapped around the small pouch.

The angel charm recipes in this book can be easily taken with you. You can put them in your pocket, purse, or place them inside your car. My friend Christopher keeps the Archangel Michael angel charm I gave him in the under seat storage compartment of his motorcycle.

You may also hold your empowered angel charms in your hands while you pray. This not only helps to supercharge your prayers but also continues to program your quartz crystal with your specific intention.

You can purchase precut, 2-inch, fabric quilting squares in many vibrant colors and brilliant patterns from fabric and craft stores as well as online. Of course, you can also cut your own squares from felt pieces or other scrap pieces of cloth you may have left over from a previous craft project.

As with the herbal sachets, the angel charm recipes suggest the use of a color that corresponds with a specific Archangel, but once again this is optional.

Archangel Color Correspondences*

Archangel Ariel: Pale or Baby Pink
Archangel Azrael: Light Beige, or Creamy White
Archangel Chamuel: Light Green
Archangel Gabriel: Golden Yellow, Copper
Archangel Haniel: Sky-Blue

Archangel Jeremiel: Deep Purple

Archangel Jophiel: Deep Pink

Archangel Metatron: Green, Violet Purple

Archangel Michael: Royal Blue, Royal Purple, Gold

Archangel Raguel: Pale Blue, or Baby Blue

Archangel Raphael: Emerald Green

Archangel Raziel: Rainbow Colors

Archangel Sandalphon: Blue-Green, Turquoise

All Archangels: White. All-purpose correspondence representing all of the archangels.

*There are many schools of thought about the color correspondence associated with the archangels. The color correspondence I have shared with you above is what I have been taught and what I personally use. Feel free to substitute any color of your choice.

Herbal Sachet Recipes

Note: All of the following ingredients listed are dried herbs and spices. To keep the fragrance at optimal, replace sachet every three months with fresh ingredients.

Archangel Michael General Protection Sachet

1 tablespoon dried orange peel
1 tablespoon frankincense

2 tablespoons sandalwood
½ cinnamon stick broken in pieces
royal purple sachet bag

General all-purpose protection sachet for the home or property.

Archangel Michael Negative Energy Repellent Sachet

1 dried bay leaf
1 tablespoon basil
1 tablespoon dill
1 tablespoon Rosemary
royal blue sachet bag

Use to ward off negative energy and unwanted spirit entities.

Archangel Gabriel Writers Inspiration Sachet

1 tablespoon lemongrass
1 tablespoon dried lemon peel
2 tablespoons dried rose petals
1 tablespoon long grain rice uncooked
3 drops rose geranium essential oil
2 drops lemon essential oil
golden yellow sachet bag

Mix rice and essential oils in a glass bowl or container, and then add dried herbs. This sachet blend is a marvelously fragrant creativity booster.

Archangel Ariel Prayer Sachet

1 cinnamon stick broken into pieces
1 tablespoon whole cloves
1 tablespoon frankincense
1 tablespoon dried orange peel
baby pink sachet bag

An all-purpose prayer sachet corresponding to all of Archangel Ariel's attributes.

Archangel Azrael Prayer Sachet

1 tablespoon patchouli
2 tablespoons sandalwood
1 tablespoon long grain rice uncooked
3 drops vanilla essential oil
light beige or creamy white sachet bag

Mix rice and vanilla essential oil in a glass bowl or container. Add dried herbs. An all-purpose prayer sachet corresponding to all of Archangel Azrael's attributes.

Archangel Chamuel Prayer Sachet

1 tablespoon cardamom
1 tablespoon dried rose petals
3 tablespoons patchouli
1 tablespoon long grain rice uncooked
2 drops rose essential oil
2 drops vanilla essential oil
light green sachet bag

Mix rice and essential oils in a glass bowl or container. Add herbs. An all-purpose prayer sachet corresponding to all of Archangel Chamuel's attributes.

Archangel Gabriel Prayer Sachet

1 tablespoon gardenia
1 tablespoon dried lemon peel
1 tablespoon myrrh
1 ½ tablespoons sandalwood
1 tablespoon long grain rice uncooked
2 drops gardenia essential oil
golden yellow sachet bag

Mix rice and gardenia essential oil in a glass bowl or container. Add herbs. An all-purpose prayer sachet corresponding to all of Archangel Gabriel's attributes.

Archangel Haniel Prayer Sachet

1 tablespoon lemongrass
2 tablespoons Jasmine
1 tablespoon long grain rice uncooked
2 drops Jasmine essential oil
sky-blue sachet bag

Mix rice and Jasmine essential oil in a glass bowl or container. Add herbs. An all-purpose prayer sachet corresponding to all of Archangel Haniel's attributes.

Archangel Jeremiel Prayer Sachet

1 tablespoon allspice
1 tablespoon basil
1 tablespoon geranium
2 tablespoons Juniper
2 tablespoons myrrh
1 tablespoon long grain rice uncooked
2 drops ginger essential oil
deep purple sachet bag

Mix rice and ginger essential oil in a glass bowl or container. Add herbs. An all-purpose prayer sachet corresponding to all of Archangel Jeremiel's attributes.

Archangel Jophiel Prayer Sachet

1 tablespoon marjoram
1 tablespoon mugwort
1 tablespoon thyme
2 tablespoons catnip
2 tablespoons dried rose petals
1 tablespoon long grain rice uncooked
1 drop spearmint essential oil
2 drops rose essential oil
deep pink sachet bag

Mix rice and essential oils in a glass bowl or container. Add herbs. An all-purpose prayer sachet corresponding to all of Archangel Jophiel's attributes.

Archangel Metatron Prayer Sachet

1 tablespoon caraway seeds
1 tablespoon mint
2 tablespoons Cypress
2 tablespoons patchouli
3 tablespoons lavender
1 tablespoon long grain rice uncooked
1 drop patchouli essential oil
2 drops lavender essential oil
green sachet bag

Mix rice and essential oils in a glass bowl or container. Add herbs. An all-purpose prayer sachet corresponding to all of Archangel Metatron's attributes.

Archangel Michael Prayer Sachet

1 tablespoon frankincense
1 tablespoon dried orange peel
1 tablespoon sandalwood
1 tablespoon long grain rice uncooked
2 drops rose geranium essential oil
gold sachet bag

Mix rice and rose geranium essential oil in a glass bowl or container. Add herbs. An all-purpose prayer sachet corresponding to all of Archangel Michael's attributes.

Archangel Raguel Prayer Sachet

1 tablespoons star anise
2 tablespoons Cedar
2 tablespoons whole cloves
3 tablespoons Rosemary
1 tablespoon long grain rice uncooked
1 drop frankincense essential oil
1 drop sandalwood essential oil
light blue sachet bag

Mix rice and essential oils in a glass bowl or container. Add herbs. An all-purpose prayer sachet corresponding to all of Archangel Raguel's attributes.

Archangel Raphael Prayer Sachet

1 tablespoon Rosemary
2 tablespoons dried rose petals
2 tablespoons sandalwood
1 tablespoon long grain rice uncooked
1 drop ginger essential oil
2 drops cinnamon essential oil
emerald green sachet bag

Mix rice and essential oils in a glass bowl or container. Add herbs. An all-purpose prayer sachet corresponding to all of Archangel Raphael's attributes.

Archangel Raziel Prayer Sachet

1 cinnamon stick broken into pieces
1 tablespoon Juniper
1 tablespoon frankincense
2 tablespoons dried orange peel
1 tablespoon long grain rice uncooked
1 drop frankincense essential oil
1 drop sweet orange essential oil
white sachet bag

Mix rice and essential oils in a glass bowl or container. Add herbs. An all-purpose prayer sachet corresponding to all of Archangel Raziel's attributes.

Archangel Sandalphon Prayer Sachet

1 tablespoon anise seeds
1 tablespoon dried lemon peel
2 tablespoons Rosemary
3 tablespoons sandalwood
1 tablespoon long grain rice uncooked
1 drop ginger essential oil
2 drops sandalwood essential oil
turquoise blue sachet bag

Mix rice and essential oils in a glass bowl or container. Add herbs. An all-purpose prayer sachet corresponding to all of Archangel Sandalphon's attributes.

Archangel Uriel Prayer Sachet

1 tablespoon whole cloves
2 tablespoons patchouli
3 tablespoons lavender
1 tablespoon long grain rice uncooked
1 drop patchouli essential oil
2 drops lavender essential oil
yellow sachet bag

Mix rice and essential oils in a glass bowl or container. Add herbs. An all-purpose prayer sachet corresponding to all of Archangel Uriel's attributes.

Archangel Zadkiel Prayer Sachet

1 tablespoon chamomile
1 tablespoon Rosemary
1 tablespoon dried rose petals
3 tablespoons sandalwood
1 tablespoon long grain rice uncooked
1 drop Roman chamomile essential oil
1 drop rose essential oil
2 drops sandalwood essential oil
dark blue sachet bag

Mix rice and essential oils in a glass bowl or container. Add herbs. An all-purpose prayer sachet corresponding to all of Archangel Zadkiel's attributes.

Archangel Ariel Prosperity Sachet

1 cinnamon stick broken into pieces
2 tablespoons whole cloves
3 tablespoons patchouli
1 tablespoon long grain rice uncooked
1 drop cinnamon essential oil
2 drops patchouli essential oil

baby pink sachet bag

Mix rice and essential oils in a glass bowl or co..
herbs. Use to draw more abundance and prosperity into your
life experience.

Archangel Raphael Sleepy Time Sachet

2 tablespoons dried rose petals
3 tablespoons chamomile
1 tablespoon long grain rice uncooked
1 drop rose geranium essential oil
2 drops Roman chamomile essential oil
white sachet bag

Mix rice and essential oils in a glass bowl or container. Add
herbs. Place near your pillow, or on your nightstand to help
promote vivid dreams.

Archangel Raguel Peaceful Home Sachet

2 tablespoons dried orange peel
3 tablespoons honeysuckle blossoms
1 tablespoon long grain rice uncooked
1 drop sweet orange essential oil
2 drops honeysuckle essential oil
light blue sachet bag

x rice and essential oils in a glass bowl or container. Add herbs. Use to promote peaceful interactions within the home environment.

Archangel Jophiel Lovely Sachet

1 tablespoon dried orange peel
1 tablespoon Rosemary
2 tablespoons dried rose petals
1 tablespoon long grain rice uncooked
1 drop Jasmine essential oil
1 drop sweet orange essential oil
2 drops rose geranium essential oil
deep pink sachet bag

Mix rice and essential oils in a glass bowl or container. Add herbs. Use wherever you would like to add a mysterious touch of sensuality. The fragrance is well . . . lovely!

Angel Charm Recipes

To assemble Angel Charms: Place a small quartz crystal in the center of a 2-inch square piece of fabric, add all dry ingredients over the crystal, place essential oils onto the cotton ball, place cotton ball on top of the herbs, and secure tightly with a string or ribbon. Add a small charm or bauble (optional).

Note: All of the following ingredients listed are dried herbs and spices. To keep the fragrance at optimal, replace angel charm every three months with fresh ingredients.

<u>Archangel Jophiel Romantic Love Charm</u>

2 teaspoons rose petals
1 teaspoon Rosemary
1 teaspoon sandalwood
1 drop rose geranium essential oil
1 drop sandalwood essential oil
cotton ball
small quartz crystal
deep pink 2-inch square piece of fabric

Use to draw romantic love.

Archangel Chamuel Job Finder Charm

3 teaspoons patchouli
2 teaspoons dried orange peel
1 teaspoon whole cloves
cotton ball
2 drops patchouli essential oil
1 drop sweet orange essential oil
small quartz crystal
light green 2-inch square piece of fabric

Used to find the job of your dreams. You can also secretly carry this with you into your next job interview.

Archangel Raguel Peaceful Resolution Charm

3 teaspoons Oak Moss
1 teaspoon whole cloves
1 teaspoon Rosemary
cotton ball
2 drops patchouli essential oil
1 drop vanilla essential oil
small quartz crystal
pale blue 2-inch square piece of fabric

Looking for peaceful resolution? With Archangel Raguel's assistance this Angel charm can help. Carry it with you during business negotiations, court cases, or in any situation where you desire a peaceful, and equitable outcome for all concerned.

Archangel Michael Courage Charm

2 teaspoons frankincense
1 teaspoon sandalwood
1 teaspoon Rosemary
cotton ball
1 drop rose geranium essential oil
1 drop vanilla essential oil
small quartz crystal
royal purple 2-inch square piece of fabric

Use to boost your courage and confidence.

Archangel Ariel Abundance Charm

1 teaspoon cinnamon
1 teaspoon whole cloves
1 teaspoon Rosemary
one cotton ball
2 drops almond essential oil
1 drop sweet orange essential oil
small quartz crystal

baby pink 2-inch square piece of fabric

Not enough money at the end of the month? Use this angel charm to create and draw to you additional sources of abundance and prosperity.

Archangel Azrael Grief Support Charm

2 teaspoons rose petals
1 teaspoon frankincense
1 teaspoon Rosemary
cotton ball
2 drops rose geranium essential oil
1 drop vanilla essential oil
small quartz crystal
off-white 2-inch square piece of fabric

Carry with you to help ease the emotional pain due to the loss of a loved one or a pet. This Angel charm gives off a sweet and comforting fragrance.

Archangel Ariel Prayer Charm

3 teaspoons Jasmine
2 teaspoons dried orange peel
cotton ball
2 drops Jasmine essential oil
1 drop sweet orange essential oil

small quartz crystal
baby pink 2-inch square piece of fabric

Corresponds with all of Archangel Ariel's attributes.

Archangel Azrael Prayer Charm

3 teaspoons sandalwood
2 teaspoons Rosemary
cotton ball
2 drops sandalwood essential oil
1 drop rose geranium essential oil
small quartz crystal
light beige or creamy white 2-inch square piece of fabric

Corresponds with all of Archangel Azrael's attributes.

Archangel Chamuel Prayer Charm

3 teaspoons Yarrow
2 teaspoons dried lemon peel
1 teaspoon Rosemary
cotton ball
2 drops rose essential oil
1 drop lemon essential oil
small quartz crystal
light green 2-inch square piece of fabric

Corresponds with all of Archangel Chamuel's attributes.

Archangel Haniel Prayer Charm

3 teaspoons sandalwood
2 teaspoons dried orange peel
1 teaspoon cinnamon
cotton ball
2 drops sandalwood essential oil
1 drop sweet orange essential oil
small quartz crystal
light blue 2-inch square piece of fabric

Corresponds with all of Archangel Haniel's attributes.

Archangel Jeremiel Prayer Charm

3 teaspoons sandalwood
1 teaspoon chamomile
1 teaspoon Rosemary
cotton ball
2 drops sandalwood essential oil
1 drop lemon essential oil
small quartz crystal
deep purple 2-inch square piece of fabric

Corresponds with all of Archangel Jeremiel's attributes.

Archangel Jophiel Prayer Charm

3 teaspoons rose petals
2 teaspoons Rosemary
cotton ball
2 drops rose geranium essential oil
1 drop vanilla essential oil
small quartz crystal
deep pink 2-inch square piece of fabric

Corresponds to all of Archangel Jophiel's attributes.

Archangel Metatron Prayer Charm

3 teaspoons Rosemary
2 teaspoons frankincense
1 teaspoon lavender
cotton ball
1 drop lavender essential oil
1 drop lemon essential oil
small quartz crystal
green 2-inch square piece of fabric

Corresponds to all of Archangel Metatron's attributes.

Archangel Michael Prayer Charm

3 teaspoons Rosemary
2 teaspoons dried orange peel
cotton ball
2 drops pine essential oil
1 drop sweet orange essential oil
small quartz crystal
royal blue 2-inch square piece of fabric

Corresponds to all of Archangel Michael's attributes.

Archangel Raguel Prayer Charm

3 teaspoons dried rose petals
2 teaspoons Rosemary
1 teaspoon whole cloves
cotton ball
2 drops rose geranium essential oil
2 drops clove essential oil
small quartz crystal
baby blue 2-inch square piece of fabric

Corresponds to all of Archangel Raguel's attributes.

Archangel Raphael Prayer Charm

3 teaspoons lavender
2 teaspoons dried lemon peel
1 teaspoon Rosemary
cotton ball
2 drops lavender essential oil
1 drop lemon essential oil
small quartz crystal
emerald green 2-inch square piece of fabric

Corresponds to all of Archangel Raphael's attributes.

Archangel Raziel Prayer Charm

3 teaspoons gardenia
2 teaspoons dried orange peel
1 teaspoon Rosemary
cotton ball
2 drops geranium essential oil
1 drop ginger essential oil
small quartz crystal
white 2-inch square piece of fabric

Corresponds with all of Archangel Raziel's attributes.

Archangel Sandalphon Prayer Charm

2 teaspoons Jasmine
1 teaspoon sandalwood
1 teaspoon dried rose petals
1 teaspoon dried orange peel
cotton ball
1 drop Jasmine essential oil
1 drop sandalwood essential oil
1 drop rose essential oil
1 drop sweet orange essential oil
small quartz crystal
turquoise blue 2-inch square piece of fabric

Corresponds with all of Archangel Sandalphon's attributes.

Archangel Uriel Prayer Charm

3 teaspoons lavender
1 teaspoon Rosemary
1 teaspoon fennel seed
cotton ball
3 drops lavender essential oil
small quartz crystal
yellow 2-inch square piece of fabric

Corresponds with all of Archangel Uriel's attributes.

<u>Archangel Zadkiel Prayer Charm</u>

3 teaspoons bergamot
1 teaspoon lemongrass
1 teaspoon dried lemon peel
cotton ball
2 drops bergamot essential oil
1 drop lemon essential oil
small quartz crystal
dark blue 2-inch square piece of fabric

Corresponds with all of Archangel Zadkiel's attributes.

Dry Potpourri Recipes

These dry potpourri recipes create small batches, perfect for a small spaces or rooms. For larger quantities, double or triple the recipes.

To assemble dry potpourri: Mix essential oils into the rock sea salt, and then add the dried herbs, tossing the mixture lightly. Display in a decorative bowl or plate.

Note: All of the following ingredients listed are dried herbs and spices. To keep the fragrance at optimal, replace your potpourri every 2 to 4 weeks. CAUTION! Keep away from children and pets. Do not eat!

Archangel Chamuel "Newness" Potpourri

3 tablespoons chamomile
3 tablespoons dried orange peel
2 tablespoons lavender
1 tablespoon rock sea salt
3 drops Roman chamomile essential oil
2 drops lavender essential oil

Use to charge the area with the energetic feeling of new opportunities and new things.

Archangel Metatron Spiritual Awareness Potpourri

3 tablespoons lavender
3 tablespoons Yarrow
2 tablespoons frankincense
1 tablespoon rock sea salt
3 drops rose essential oil
1 drop lavender essential oil

For increased spiritual awareness place a bowl or dish of this heavenly potpourri in your meditation or yoga room.

Archangel Jophiel Happy Heart Potpourri

4 tablespoons dried orange peel
4 tablespoons lavender

1 tablespoon rock sea salt
4 drops apple blossom essential oil

Use to create a happy and joyful ambience.

Archangel Ariel Prosperity Potpourri

3 tablespoons Cedar chips
3 tablespoons whole cloves
3 cinnamon sticks broken into pieces
3 tablespoons dried orange peel
1 tablespoon rock sea salt
3 drops cinnamon essential oil
2 drops clove essential oil
2 drops ginger essential oil

A fragrant, woodsy potpourri sure to remind you of the abundance and prosperity you already have.

Archangel Michael Negativity Purging Potpourri

3 tablespoons Cedar chips
3 tablespoons pine chips
small handful of pine needles (optional)
a few small pine cones (optional)
2 tablespoons rock sea salt
4 drops cedarwood essential oil
2 drops eucalyptus essential oil

Use to purge the room of negativity.

Archangel Jophiel Just "Rosy" Romantic Potpourri

4 tablespoons dried rose petals
2 tablespoons dried orange peel
1 tablespoon rock sea salt
4 drops rose essential oil
2 drops sweet orange essential oil

Use to set a romantic tone in your living space.

Archangel Gabriel Creative Illumination Potpourri

3 tablespoons lemongrass
2 tablespoons Rosemary
1 tablespoon thyme
1 tablespoon dried lemon peel
1 Bay leaf crushed
1 tablespoon rock sea salt
4 drops lemon essential oil

Use to wake up your creative faculties.

Archangel Chamuel Find New Love Potpourri

2 tablespoons dried rose petals
2 tablespoons Jasmine
1 tablespoon basil
1 teaspoon crushed anise seed
1 teaspoon crushed coriander
1 tablespoon rock sea salt
4 drops Jasmine essential oil

Use to remind yourself of your intention to find and to discover a romantic partner.

Archangel Jeremiel Clairvoyance Potpourri

3 tablespoons dried rose petals
2 tablespoons chamomile
1 Bay leaf crushed
1 cinnamon stick broken into pieces
½ teaspoon allspice
½ teaspoon clove powder
1 tablespoon rock sea salt
3 drops rose geranium essential oil
2 drops vanilla essential oil

Use to awaken your third eye. For all of you Angel card readers - place a small bowl of this third eye strengthening potpourri in your reading room!

Archangel Raphael Healing Potpourri

3 tablespoons lavender
1 tablespoon mint
1 tablespoon thyme
1 tablespoon basil
1 teaspoon ground cloves
1 teaspoon caraway seeds crushed
1 tablespoon rock salt
4 drops lavender essential oil

Use to fill your space with a healing, soothing, and peaceful ambiance.

Prayer Water

The use of consecrated water to heal and to bless people and objects has been practiced for thousands of years. Consecrated water is associated with baptism, clearing negativity, rebirth, and spiritual purification.

Virtually all religions of the past and many spiritual traditions of the present age use consecrated water; water which has been infused with the intent to heal and to bless.

The effectiveness of the use of consecrated water is also scientifically viable. In his book Messages in Water, Masaru Emoto theorized that human consciousness has an effect on the molecular structure of the body. His work explores his belief that water could react to positive words and thoughts, and that polluted water could be cleansed through positive visualization and thinking.

Prayer water adds an additional component which greatly magnifies the intensity and effectiveness of water do to one "secret" ingredient. The secret ingredient is . . . drumroll please . . . salt! Yep! Surprising right?

The reason that salt is so effective is because it is made of a crystalline structure. Crystals have the ability to receive an imprint of your desired intention that affects both the physical and spirit world.

Like that of a quartz crystal, salt can be programmed through the spoken word, or through emotionalized thoughts.

How to Use Prayer Water

The prayer water recipes shared in this chapter are designed to help you magnify your prayers, to bless and heal yourself and others, and to also consecrate any herb or oil recipes you have made.

To bless and consecrate the water, you would simply use the empowering right found in chapter 2 of this book, *How to Energetically Empower Your Recipes.*

To give you recipes and added energetic boost spray your hands with a prayer water that corresponds with your recipe of intent, and then perform the empowering right. Alternatively, you may also use the basic prayer water recipe which serves an all-purpose function.

You may use the basic prayer water recipe to by sprinkling (or lightly spraying) a few drops onto the sick, or around your living space to cleanse, clear, and lift any dissonant energies.

Prayer water recipes are also very effective when sprayed on the body's pulse points, and are also intended to help you connect with the vibration of each specific Archangel.

Basic Prayer Water Recipe

This recipe is an all-purpose blessed holy water which you can use for anything.

- 1 cup of room temperature spring water
- 1 tablespoon of sea salt
- a decorative bottle or jar to store

Important! Keep out of reach from children and pets. Do not drink this mixture or any of the other prayer water recipes!

Aromatic Prayer Water Recipes

The following are general purpose aromatic prayer waters. Shake well before each use. Store in an 8-ounce glass jar or bottle. Keep out of reach from children and pets. Do not drink!

Archangel Michael Protective Holy Water ⚔

1 tablespoon sea salt
1 cup spring water
decorative jar or bottle to store

To transmute and dissolve negative energy sprinkle around the home.

Archangel Ariel Aromatic Prayer Water

2 drops ginger essential oil
6 drops orange essential oil
10 drops honeysuckle essential oil
1 tablespoon sea salt
1 cup spring water

General prayer water corresponding to all of Archangel Ariel's attributes - material needs, abundance, prosperity, healing and protecting the environment and wildlife.

Archangel Azrael Aromatic Prayer Water

8 drops rose or rose geranium essential oil
10 drops vanilla essential oil
1 tablespoon sea salt
1 cup spring water

General prayer water corresponding to all of Archangel Azrael's attributes - emotional healing, and to promote healing and support for grief over the loss of a loved one or pet.

Archangel Chamuel Aromatic Prayer Water

6 drops patchouli essential oil
12 drops neroli essential oil

1 tablespoon sea salt
1 cup spring water

General prayer water corresponding to all of Archangel
Chamuel's attributes - to find any lost item, to finding new
love, a new job, new friends, a new home, and relationship
healing.

Archangel Gabriel Aromatic Prayer Water

2 drops sweet orange essential oil
6 drops sandalwood essential oil
10 drops Jasmine essential oil
1 tablespoon sea salt
1 cup spring water

General prayer water corresponding to all of Archangel
Gabriel's attributes - wisdom, confident decision-making,
creative illumination, intelligence, and communication.

Archangel Haniel Aromatic Prayer Water

3 drops gardenia essential oil
3 drops sweet orange essential oil
6 drops sandalwood essential oil
6 drops tonka bean essential oil
1 tablespoon sea salt
1 cup spring water

General prayer water corresponding to all of Archangel Haniel's attributes - psychic awareness, peace, joy, harmony, creative inspiration, increasing productivity, meditation, and spirituality.

Archangel Jeremiel Aromatic Prayer Water

4 drops Jasmine essential oil
4 drops rose or rose geranium essential oil
10 drops sandalwood essential oil
1 tablespoon sea salt
1 cup spring water

General prayer water corresponding to all of Archangel Jeremiel's attributes - life purpose, problem-solving, clairvoyant dreams and visions, divine wisdom, spiritual wisdom, and spiritual awakening.

Archangel Jophiel Prayer Water

4 drops sweet orange essential oil
4 drops ylang-ylang essential oil
10 drops patchouli essential oil
1 tablespoon sea salt
1 cup spring water

A general prayer water corresponding to all of Archangel Jophiel's attributes - love, happiness, beauty, fertility, abundance, creativity, positive thinking and feeling, clearing subconscious clutter.

Archangel Metatron Prayer Water

4 drops bergamot essential oil
4 drops lavender essential oil
10 drops rose or rose geranium essential oil
1 tablespoon sea salt
1 cup spring water

A general prayer water corresponding to all of Archangel Metatron's attributes - spiritual growth, spiritual awareness, and spiritual and personal power.

Archangel Michael Prayer Water

8 drops frankincense essential oil
8 drops sandalwood essential oil
2 drops sweet orange essential oil
1 tablespoon sea salt
1 cup spring water

A general prayer water corresponding to all of Archangel Michael's attributes - courage, confidence, protection of any kind, purification, releasing of negative energy, and discovering life purpose.

Archangel Raguel Prayer Water

4 drops clove essential oil
6 drops rosemary essential oil
8 drops Clary Sage essential oil
1 tablespoon sea salt
1 cup spring water

A general prayer water corresponding to all of Archangel Raguel's attributes - justice, fairness, resolution to legal matters, restoring harmony relationships, resolving conflicts, and healing of arguments and misunderstandings.

Archangel Raphael Prayer Water

7 drops rose or rose geranium essential oil
7 drops lavender essential oil
4 drops frankincense essential oil
1 tablespoon sea salt
1 cup spring water

A general prayer water corresponding to all of Archangel Raphael's attributes - physical, emotional, mental, and spiritual healing, health, purification, healing of relationships, and healing of animals and pets

Archangel Raziel Prayer Water

6 drops cedarwood essential oil
6 drops frankincense essential oil
6 drops sandalwood essential oil
1 tablespoon sea salt
1 cup spring water

A general prayer water corresponding to all of Archangel Raziel's attributes - manifestation of desires, abundance, prosperity, working with Universal Law, lucid dreaming, dream interpretation, and spiritual wisdom.

Archangel Sandalphon Prayer Water

2 drops Cedarwood essential oil
6 drops myrrh
10 drops frankincense
1 tablespoon sea salt
1 cup spring water

A general prayer water corresponding to all of Archangel Sandalphon attributes – supercharged prayer, peace and serenity in difficult times, dispelling fear, and grounding.

Archangel Uriel Prayer Water

2 drops lavender essential oil
6 drops thyme essential oil
10 drops peppermint essential oil
1 tablespoon sea salt
1 cup spring water

A general prayer water corresponding to all of Archangel Uriel's attributes - spiritual wisdom, insight, and illumination, mental clarification, problem-solving, and creative ideas.

Archangel Zadkiel Prayer Water

6 drops bergamot essential oil
6 drops rose or rose geranium essential oil
6 drops ylang-ylang
1 tablespoon sea salt
1 cup spring water

A general prayer water corresponding to all of Archangel Zadkiel's attributes - unconditional forgiveness, compassion, healing of painful memories, and relationship healing.

Prayers for Specific Needs

The simple prayers in this section are optional and are just suggestions. God and the angels do not require canned prayers. The only thing they require is that you ask from your heart, and that is what prayer is about.

When it comes to prayer the most important thing is to ask for what you need or want clearly and succinctly. This means short, sweet, and direct requests. And no worries − 'Thee's' and 'Thou's' are not necessary.

The word prayer comes from the Latin word 'precari' which means to ask in earnest. In other words, to ask from your heart. Feel free to add or subtract from these prayers as you see fit. Also feel free to add whatever ending that you are most comfortable with such as: 'And so it is!' or 'Amen', etc.

When it comes to prayer I'm often asked, "Is it wrong to pray to the Archangel's?" Or, "Can I pray directly to God instead?" And so on and so forth.

My answer is to just pray the way your most comfortable, and according to your own spiritual tradition instead of getting all tangled up in religious dogma. The most important thing is to ask.

The Archangel's are God's helpers, and when you ask for their help you are asking for God's help.

Prayers for Various Needs

Abundance

Archangel Ariel,

I am so happy and grateful for the continuous showering of abundance in my life, which comes in easy and effortless ways. May my prosperity and abundance go forth and bloom so that my overflow will bless others, as well as to joyfully support my life's passion and purpose.

Thank you! And so it is! Amen.

Beautifying Your Thoughts

Archangel Jophiel,

Beautify my mind and thoughts. May you help me to discern those thoughts and beliefs that no longer serve my highest good, replacing them with productive, fragrant thoughts.

I know that emotionalized thought creates my reality, so empower my mind to always think and believe the best, and highest thoughts in every area of my life, and to always respond to life through the eyes of love.

Thank you! And so it is! Amen.

Blessing Your Marriage

Archangel Jophiel,

Bless my marriage. Thank you for [name of spouse]. Help to keep our passion alive, and our love for one another new.

Keep at the forefront of my mind all of the good qualities she/he captured my heart with when we first met and help me to overlook those qualities that may at times annoy me.

For I know these lower qualities are just a reflection of what I need to work on in myself. Help me to be willing to love anyways, and to work on healing myself of those lesser qualities for the benefit of a loving, healthy, happy, and lifelong relationship with my spouse.

Thank you! And so it is! Amen.

Clairaudience

Archangel Zadkiel,

For the highest good of all concerned open my ear chakras so that I can hear intuitive wisdom and guidance with crystal clear clarity.

Thank you! And so it is! Amen.

Clairsentience

Archangel Raguel,

May the warmth of your love surround me. Fill me with Divine Light and allow me to clearly feel the wisdom and guidance that God and the Angels wish to impart to me.

Thank you! And so it is! Amen.

Clairvoyance

Archangel Raziel,

Open my third eye and fill it with Divine Light. Thank you for continuing to illuminate my inner knowing so that I can clearly see and receive intuitive messages for the highest good of all concerned.

And so it is! Amen.

Clairvoyant Dreams

Archangel Jeremiel,

Allow me to receive Divine Wisdom concerning [subject] through my dreams. Please make the information you provide me with clear, and easy for me to understand, and/or interpret, and also and also allow me to easily remember your guidance when I awake.

Thank you! And so it is! Amen.

Clear Decision-Making

Archangel Gabriel,

Give me the wisdom to make a clear and accurate decision concerning [decision you must make]. It is my intention with your guidance to make a decision that benefits the highest good of everyone involved.

Thank you! And so it is! Amen.

Clearing of Arguments and Misunderstandings

Archangel Gabriel,

Clear away the argument/misunderstanding about [issue that needs to be resolved]. May all parties involved be willing to look at this situation with a new perspective, and through the eyes of Divine Love. For the highest good of everyone concerned, may all parties be willing to let this go in Love and Light.

Thank you! And so it is! Amen.

Conception of a Child

Archangel Gabriel,

It is my heartfelt intention to conceive a child. Please bless my womb so that I am fertile. Surround me within your protective bubble of copper light, and eliminate any thoughts or beliefs that may hinder me from conceiving a happy healthy child.

Thank you! And so it is! Amen.

Courage and Confidence

Archangel Michael,

Fill me right now with the courage and confidence I need to [reason]. May you and your band of holy warriors continue to stand beside me, behind me, and in front of me, supporting me and lifting me up in every way.

Thank you! And so it is! Amen.

Creative Ideas

Archangel Jophiel,

Illuminate my mind with creative ideas for my [art project, book project, etc.]. I know that all creativity is God-breathed so I open my heart and my mind to receive your creative inspirations clearly right now.

Thank you! And so it is! Amen.

Creative Illumination for Artists and Writers

Archangel Gabriel,

Illuminate me with creativity and clarity so that I can quickly
and easily create Divine masterpieces of art, and/or with the
written word. Bless my creative endeavors which have been
God breathed. May my creative energy be well accepted by
others, as well as benefit the minds and hearts of all who
have been touched by my creative projects.

Thank you! And so it is! Amen.

Discovering Your Life Purpose

Archangel Michael,

I feel a yearning in my heart, a deep knowing that I have a
mission to fulfill here on earth. Please give me the clarity and
peace of mind about what my next step is so that I can
lovingly step into my life's purpose.

Thank you! And so it is! Amen.

Dispelling Fear and Worry

Archangel Sandalphon,

Release my fear and anxiety over [situation causing fear and worry]. I am aware that the acronym for FEAR means, False – Evidence – Appearing - Real.

Help me now to stay present and to look at the truth of the situation from your loving perspective. I am affirming a positive outcome in the situation right now, and willingly roll the situation into the arms of the Divine to resolve in a manner that benefits everyone concerned.

Thank you! And so it is! Amen.

Dream Visitation from Loved Ones in Heaven or Your Guardian Angels

Archangel Azrael,

Tonight I would like a dream visitation by [name of person]. Allow me to be alert when he/she appears, and receptive to their messages. Above all, awaken me after their visit, and allow me to vividly remember the dream and their messages to me.

Thank you! And so it is! Amen.

Favorable Legal Outcomes

Archangel Raguel,

It is my intention to have a fair and equitable outcome regarding [legal situation]. I know that God is a God of fairness, so I ask that this legal matter be resolved in a manner that is fair and just for all parties concerned.

Thank you! And so it is! Amen.

Finding a New Home

Archangel Chamuel,

Thank you for leading me/us to the perfect home, at the perfect price, located in an area that best supports my needs/the needs of our family. May only love, joy, and peace flourish within the walls of my new living space.

Thank you! And so it is! Amen.

Finding Love

Archangel Chamuel,

Point me in the direction of my true love; a relationship that is mutually respectful, socially and sexually compatible, and one that positively and mutually supports the goals and dreams of one another. May you enrich our lives in the fullness of God's love now and forever.

Thank you! And so it is! Amen.

Forgiveness

Archangel Zadkiel,

Please help me to forgive [person/persons] for [what you wish to forgive]. I am not condoning what has been done, but I'm willing to let it go and to forgive all parties involved, including myself and the role I have played in the situation.

For I know everyone does the best they can do with the knowledge and understanding they have at the time. And with that understanding, I release this to you now and forever.

Thank you! And so it is! Amen.

General Psychic Awareness

Archangel Haniel,

Open my intuitive centers so that I can clearly receive messages from God and the Angels right now. I am ready and receptive to receive your loving guidance.

Thank you! And so it is! Amen.

General Success

Archangel Ariel,

Continue to bless my [fill in the blank, i.e. business, project, etc.] with massive success. Give me the clarity and confidence I need to continue to take the inspired action steps I need to follow through. Bring into my experience all the people and resources I need to succeed.

Thank you! And so it is! Amen.

Grief over the Death of a Loved One

Archangel Azrael,

My heart aches over the loss of [person's name]. Although I know he/she is safe in heaven, the emotional pain of their departure is very deep.

Help me to remember the wonderful and joyous times we shared together, for these memories help to keep them alive in my mind and in my heart.

Give me signs from heaven that they are okay and at peace. Help me to honor my tears, and surround me with your loving presence when my grief overtakes me.

Thank you! And so it is! Amen.

Grief over the Loss of a Pet

Archangel Azrael,

My heart is broken! My beloved pet [name of pet] is gone and I miss him/her terribly. Please surround me with love and understanding as I/we move through this emotional time.

Thank you for choosing me/us to love and care for [name of pet]. It was an extreme honor.

Give me/us heavenly signs that [name of pet] is safe and at peace, and remind me/us of your supportive presence when my grief overtakes me with tears.

Thank you! And so it is! Amen.

Healing of Addictions

Archangel Raphael,

Release me from my addiction to [addiction or habit]. Remove all desire and cravings for the substance. This habit no longer serves my highest good, and I willingly let it go right now.

Help me to establish new thoughts and habits that support me in every way, and continue to give me the strength each day to live free from this substance. Strengthen me with God's love, fortitude, and peace.

Thank you! And so it is! Amen.

Healing of Mind and Emotions

Archangel Raphael,

Release my mind from excessive thoughts of worry, and lift and heal any emotions that are weighing me down; such as fear and confusion. Replace these thoughts with confidence, joy, and hope.

I willingly let go of any thoughts and emotions that no longer serve me, and instead choose loving and empowering thoughts and emotions that resonate with love.

Thank you! And so it is! Amen.

Help Finding a Lost Item

Archangel Chamuel,

I know that nothing is lost in the mind of God. Please give me a clear and open mind and lead me/us to my/our [name of the lost object].

Thank you! And so it is! Amen.

Help with Studying and Tests

Archangel Uriel,

Sharpen my mind and allow me to absorb this material quickly and easily. Provide me with ways to learn this material that is fun and enjoyable, and supercharge my memory so that I can complete my exams with top marks.

Thank you! And so it is! Amen.

Increase Productivity

Archangel Haniel,

Increased productivity means more time, money, and joy. It is my heartfelt intention to be more productive in the area of [area you would like to be more productive]. Give me a clear and organized mind and help me to be clear about the end result I am looking for. Supply me with the energy to follow through so that I will take the action steps necessary towards completion of my tasks.

Thank you! And so it is! Amen.

Manifesting a Goal

Archangel Raziel,

It is my clear intention to manifest [goal/desire] into my life experience in a fast and enjoyable way, and in a way that benefits everyone involved. I trust that what I want will be delivered to me and God's perfect timing and in God's perfect ways.

Thank you! And so it is! Amen.

Money for Particular Need

Archangel Ariel,

It is my intention to manifest [exact amount of money you need] into my life experience on or before [date]. This money is necessary for [why you need it]. I release my request to you now for I know that you are aware of my needs and that you will deliver my request in a timely manner, and in a way that benefits everyone concerned.

Thank you! And so it is! Amen.

Mutual Marriage Reconciliation

Archangel Zadkiel,

Cover us with God's love and fill us with patience and understanding as we recommit our love to one another.

Remind us to let go of the past and to instead focus on building and strengthening our love for one another day by day. May we continue forward each day by honoring and respecting each other with loving words and loving actions.

Thank you! And so it is! Amen.

New Friends

Archangel Chamuel,

Surround me with new and supported friendships with people of like minds. As loving friends may we continue to encourage, support, laugh, comfort, and teach one another, as only good friends do.

Thank you! And so it is! Amen.

New Job

Archangel Chamuel,

Guide me to gainful employment that not only pays me great wages but one that is also an enjoyable place to work. Help me to be open and perceptive to your leading.

I trust that will be led to work and a work environment that is a good fit for me, and I also trust that will come to me in God's perfect timing and perfect ways.

Thank you! And so it is! Amen.

Peace and Serenity in Difficult Times

Archangel Sandalphon,

Help me/us to stay rooted and grounded in peace and love during this difficult time. Comfort me/us with the truth that God loves me/us and is a very present source of help when things in life go awry.

I/we trust that you will create the perfect solution or outcome in regards to the situation in a way that benefits all concerned.

Thank you! And so it is! Amen.

Peaceful Interactions with Others

Archangel Raguel,

Create a spirit of peace and cooperation in this situation. Allow all parties to stay emotionally present and cooperative. Dissolve any ego-based discord and replace it with love and clarity in a way that benefits everyone concerned.

Thank you! And so it is! Amen.

Pet Healing

Archangel Raphael,

Release this illness from my beloved pet right now! Bless him/her with your divine healing light, and supercharge my pet's ability to receive your healing energy so that every cell in his/her body returns to a state of healthy vibrancy.

Thank you! And so it is! Amen.

Physical Healing

Archangel Raphael,

Restore my/name of person's body to its original state of health right now. I acknowledge that my/his/her original state of being is one of health and wholeness, and I release any thoughts, beliefs, or any other thing that is blocking me/him/her from returning to vibrant health.

I see myself/name of person as being perfect whole and complete right now!

Thank you! And so it is! Amen.

Problem-Solving

Archangel Jeremiel,

Illuminate me with Divine Wisdom so that I can discover a creative solution regarding [problem you wish to re-solve]. I know that God is the source of infinite wisdom and I allow myself to receive the solution I need in an easy and effortless manner.

Thank you! And so it is! Amen.

Protection of Family or Loved Ones

Archangel Michael,

Surround me/my family [or name of a particular person] with your brilliant sword of light. Watch and guide me/him/her/them/name of person in all our ways. Thank you for protecting me/him/her/them/name of person and bringing me/him/her/them/name of person home safely.

Thank you! And so it is! Amen.

Protection of Property

Archangel Michael,

Protect this property from all harm. Surround it, and seal it with the peace of your protective love right now!

Thank you! And so it is! Amen.

Purify Your Living Space

Archangel Michael,

It is my intention to cleanse, clear, and to purify this living space from all negativity. Release any dissonant energies from this place right now, and fill it with God's Divine Light. May only peace and love abide within these walls from this day forward.

Thank you! And so it is! Amen.

Relationship Breakup

Archangel Michael,

It is time for this relationship to end for the good of everyone concerned. With your brilliant sword of blue light please cut the energetic cords that connect us.

Give us both a spirit of cooperation, as it is my intention that this transition is smooth for the both of us. Please surround us both with love, compassion, and understanding as we go our separate ways.

Thank you! And so it is! Amen.

Restoring Harmony in Relationships

Archangel Raguel,

Restore harmony in my relationship(s) with [name/names], and surround us with love and light. Help us to always remember that only love is real and to always seek love first in every interaction we have together.

Thank you! And so it is! Amen.

Romantic Love

Archangel Jophiel,

Spice up my relationship with [name], providing us with fun and playful ways to explore romance and sexual passion. Allow this fiery passion to deepen our soul connection to each other by immersing us in the deepest and most intimate form of love.

Thank you! And so it is! Amen.

Safe Travel

Archangel Michael,

Place your protective shield around me/us right now as we travel to [your destination]. May my/our trip go smoothly, and may it be enjoyable. Thank you in advance for my/our safe arrival.

Thank you! And so it is! Amen

Sale of a Home

Archangel Raziel,

Thank you for the gift of this home. It is now time for me/us to move on so I asked that you bless this house in preparation it for its next owners. Fill this house up with the noticeable vibration of your Divine Love.

I/we ask for a quick and equitable sale of this house and affirm that everything flows smoothly in a way that supports all parties involved.

Thank you! And so it is! Amen.

Self-Forgiveness

Archangel Zadkiel,

Out of my humanness, I realize that there will be times in my life when I make mistakes. At those times, and at this present time, help me to remember that I'm not perfect, nor do I need to be.

I'm willing to forgive myself for my errors for I know that I have done the very best I could have done in regards to this situation. Help me to glean the loving lessons that the situation has brought to me so that I can learn and grow from it.

I love and honor myself and I give myself permission to be imperfect, and more importantly to use what I have learned from the situation to empower myself and my life.
Thank you! And so it is! Amen.

Spiritual and Intuitive Insight concerning a Specific Issue

Archangel Uriel,

Illuminate me with Divine Light and Wisdom. Give me the clarity and intuitive insights I need in regards to the situation right now, and give me the confidence to act on your guidance for the benefit of all concerned. Thank you! And so it is! Amen.

Spiritual Growth and Insight

Archangel Metatron,

Give me the insight I need to discern the personal characteristics God wishes to strengthen and develop in me so that I may continue to expand and grow spiritually. Bless me with continued spiritual insight so that I may promote love, light, and peace wherever I go.

Help me to always be aware of my thoughts, actions, and reactions and may you sprinkle them with Divine Love.

Thank you! And so it is! Amen.

Spiritual Protection

Archangel Michael,

Guard and protect me against the effects of fear as well as from any negative, fear-based energies. Shield me from lower based energies wherever I go, and fill me with God's protective peace.

Thank you! And so it is! Amen.

To Avert a Natural Disaster

Archangel Uriel,

Defender of the earth, may you command this [form of the potential natural disaster] to pass us by, or reduce its potential threat and magnitude for the benefit of all concerned. Keep all of your creation safe and secure in the illumination of God's Love and Light.

Thank you! And so it is! Amen.

To Promote Joy and Happiness

Archangel Haniel,

I'm willing to see the bright side in everything for I know that happiness is a choice. Every day in all your wonderful ways surround me with more and more laughter, happy people, joyful thoughts, and fun experiences. May God's love and joy emanate from me wherever I may go.

Thank you! And so it is! Amen.

Vibrant Health

Archangel Raphael,

Thank you for filling my body with continuous vibrant health. Bless every cell and molecule in my body with wholeness.

May I be balanced with sound mind and body from this day forward and forever!

Thank you! And so it is! Amen.

When a Loved One Is Dying

Archangel Azrael,

Welcome, [name's] spirit into your loving arms. May his/her transition be peaceful and gentle, and may she/he be welcomed with joy by those who have gone before her/him. Surround him/her now with your loving presence and comfort his/her family and loved ones in these final moments of life.

Thank you! And so it is! Amen.

Appendix – Archangel Attributes & Correspondences

Archangel Ariel

Recipes for abundance, prosperity, all material needs such as money, food, shelter, etc. Protecting and healing the environment and wildlife.

Allspice	Honeysuckle
Almond	Jasmine
Basil	Lavender
Bergamot Mint	Nutmeg
Calamus	Mint
Carnation	Musk
Cedar	Orange
Cinnamon	Patchouli
Clove	Peppermint
Cumin	Pine
Ginger	Rosemary
Fennel	Sage
Frankincense	Sassafras

Archangel Azrael

Recipes to promote healing and support for grief over the loss of a loved one or pet, emotional healing.

Benzoin

Chamomile

Comfrey

Cypress

Honeysuckle

Frankincense

Magnolia

Mugwort

Myrrh

Orange

Rose

Rose Geranium

Rosemary

Patchouli

Sandalwood

Valerian

Vanilla

Archangel Chamuel

Recipes to promote patience, finding new love, a new job, new home, new friends, or any lost item, relationship healing.

Apple Blossom	Lime
Basil	Lilac
Chamomile	Magnolia
Cardamom	Marjoram
Catnip	Neroli
Cinnamon	Orange
Clove	Orchid
Coriander	Patchouli
Cumin	Peppermint
Daisy	Plumeria
Dill	Rose
Ginger	Rosemary
Gardenia	Sandalwood
Rose Geranium	Sweet Pea
Hibiscus	Thyme
Honeysuckle	Vanilla
Jasmine	Violet
Lavender	Yarrow
Lemon	Ylang-Ylang

Archangel Gabriel

Recipes to promote communication, wisdom, confidence in decision-making, clearing away of confusion, creative illumination, intelligence.

Almond	Lemon
Benzoin	Lemon Verbena
Bergamot Mint	Lemongrass
Calamus	Lilac
Caraway	Lime
Cedar	Orange
Dill	Rose
Eucalyptus	Rosemary
Fennel	Peppermint
Gardenia	Sage
Grapefruit	Sandalwood
Jasmine	Thyme
Lavender	

Archangel Haniel

Recipes to promote joy, peace, psychic awareness, harmony, creative inspiration, increasing productivity, spirituality, meditation.

Anise	Lime
Apple Blossom	Mace
Bay	Marigold
Camphor	Mugwort
Catnip	Myrrh
Cedar	Nutmeg
Cinnamon	Orange
Clove	Peppermint
Coconut	Poppy Seed
Gardenia	Rose
Grapefruit	Rosemary
Frankincense	Sage
Jasmine	Sandalwood
Lemon	Tonka Bean
Lemongrass	Thyme
Lilac	Yarrow

Archangel Jeremiel

Clairvoyant dreams and visions, life purpose, problem-solving, spiritual awakening, divine wisdom, spiritual vision.

Allspice
Apple Blossom
Basil
Catnip
Chamomile
Clove
Cumin
Eucalyptus
Gardenia
Geranium
Ginger
Heather
Jasmine

Juniper
Lemon
Lilac
Lily
Pine
Rose
Rosemary
Sandalwood
Spearmint
Thyme
Vanilla
Violet

Archangel Jophiel

Recipes to promote love, beauty, happiness, fertility, creativity, abundance, positive thinking and feeling, clearing subconscious clutter.

Apple Blossom
Basil
Benzoin
Cardamom
Catnip
Cinnamon
Chamomile
Clove
Coriander
Cumin
Daisy
Dill
Gardenia
Geranium
Ginger
Heather
Hibiscus
Jasmine
Juniper
Lavender

Lilac
Magnolia
Marjoram
Mugwort
Orchid
Orange
Orris Root
Plumeria
Rose
Rosemary
Sandalwood
Spearmint
St. John's Wort
Sweet Pea
Tansy
Thyme
Vanilla
Violet
Ylang Ylang

Archangel Metatron

Recipes to promote personal and spiritual power, spiritual awareness, spiritual growth.

Almond	Lemon
Bay	Lily
Bergamot Mint	Mace
Caraway	Marjoram
Cinnamon	Mint
Cypress	Myrrh
Dill	Patchouli
Fennel	Peppermint
Frankincense	Pine
Gardenia	Rose
Geranium	Rosemary
Honeysuckle	Sage
Jasmine	Sandalwood
Lavender	Thyme
Lemongrass	Yarrow

Archangel Michael

Recipes to promote protection of any kind, releasing of negative energy, purification, courage, confidence, life purpose, and personal power.

Aloe	Garlic
Anise	Ginger
Allspice	Juniper
Angelica	Lavender
Basil	Marigold
Bay	Myrrh
Calamus	Nutmeg
Camphor	Oakmoss
Carnation	Orange
Cedar	Peppermint
Cinnamon	Pine
Clove	Rosemary
Coriander	Rose Geranium
Cumin	Saffron
Dill	Sandalwood
Eucalyptus	Thyme
Fennel	Tobacco
Frankincense	

Archangel Raguel

Recipes to promote resolution to legal matters, justice, fairness, healing arguments and misunderstandings, restoring harmony in relationships, resolving conflicts.

Anise	Oakmoss
Carnation	Orange
Cedar	Rose
Clove	Rosemary
Frankincense	Sage
Ginger	Sassafras
Honeysuckle	St. John's Wort
Juniper	Tonka Bean
Nutmeg	Vanilla

Archangel Raphael

Recipes to promote purification, health, healing in all forms – physically, emotionally, mentally, spiritually, as well as that of relationships, and animals and pets.

Aloe	Lemongrass
Allspice	Lime
Angelica	Mugwort
Bay	Myrrh
Carnation	Orange
Cedar	Pepper, Cayenne
Calamus	Peppermint
Cinnamon	Pine
Coriander	Rose
Eucalyptus	Rosemary
Fennel	Saffron
Frankincense	Sandalwood
Gardenia	Sassafras
Grapefruit	Spearmint
Lavender	Thyme
Honeysuckle	Violet
Juniper	Wintergreen
Lemon	Yerba Santa

Archangel Raziel

Recipes to promote abundance, prosperity, spiritual wisdom, manifestation of desires, lucid dreaming, dream interpretation.

Allspice
Bay
Bergamot Mint
Camphor
Carnation
Cedar
Cinnamon
Clove
Dill
Frankincense
Gardenia
Ginger
Honeysuckle
Jasmine
Juniper
Mint

Mugwort
Musk
Nutmeg
Oakmoss
Orange
Patchouli
Peppermint
Pine
Rose
Rosemary
Sage
Saffron
Sandalwood
Tangerine
Thyme
Vanilla

Archangel Sandalphon

Recipes to promote supercharged prayer, dispelling fear, peace and serenity in difficult times, grounding.

Allspice

Anise

Catnip

Chamomile

Clove

Eucalyptus

Gardenia

Geranium

Ginger

Frankincense

Honeysuckle

Jasmine

Lavender

Lemon

Lily

Marjoram

Nutmeg

Orange

Rose

Rosemary

Sage

Sandalwood

Sarsaparilla

Sassafras

St. John's Wort

Sweet Pea

Thyme

Violet

Archangel Uriel

Recipes for spiritual illumination, wisdom, and insight, creative ideas, clarification, problem-solving.

Almond	Juniper
Benzoin	Lavender
Clove	Mace
Comfrey	Patchouli
Cypress	Peppermint
Dill	Pine
Fennel	Rosemary
Frankincense	Thyme

Archangel Zadkiel

Recipes to promote compassion, relationship healing, unconditional forgiveness, healing of painful memories.

Almond
Anise
Apple Blossom
Bergamot Mint
Chamomile
Catnip
Comfrey
Dill
Eucalyptus
Gardenia
Heather
Iris
Jasmine
Lavender
Lemon
Lemongrass
Lilac

Lily
Mace
Orange
Orris Root
Parsley
Peppermint
Rose
Rosemary
Sandalwood
Spearmint
Sweet Pea
Tansy
Thyme
Vanilla
Violet
Ylang Ylang

Author Bio

I am an author, and a blogger who enjoys creating content for awesome people (just like you) who are interested in strengthening their psychic abilities and learning more about how to deepen their connection with their Angels and Spirit Guides.

I'm based in Lake Elsinore, California with a penchant for writing non-fiction 'how-to' books + reading and writing paranormal novellas + wine tasting + cooking up some incredible vegetarian cuisine.

For articles on angel communication and psychic development join me at www.DarPayment.com.

If you are interested in my intuitive services please feel free to view my business website here: www.Whispers-From-Heaven.com.

Made in the USA
Columbia, SC
03 December 2020